The Book of
EDALE

Portrait of a High Peak Village

THE EDALE SOCIETY

HALSGROVE

First published in Great Britain in 2003.

Copyright © 2003 The Edale Society.

All rights reserved. No part of this publication may be reproduced, stored in a retrieval system, or transmitted in any form or by any means without the prior permission of the copyright holder.

British Library Cataloguing-in-Publication Data.
A CIP record for this title is available from the British Library.

ISBN 1 84114 245 X

HALSGROVE

Halsgrove House
Lower Moor Way
Tiverton, Devon EX16 6SS
Tel: 01884 243242
Fax: 01884 243325
email: sales@halsgrove.com
website: www.halsgrove.com

Frontispiece photograph: *Jack Burdikin and horse-drawn mower in the Church Cottage field, c.1950s.*

Printed and bound by CPI Press, Bath.

Whilst every care has been taken to ensure the accuracy of the information contained in this book, the publisher disclaims responsibility for any mistakes which may have been inadvertently included.

Contents

	Acknowledgements	4
	Introduction	5
Chapter One:	EARLY EDALE	7
Chapter Two:	FARMS AND FARMING	11
Chapter Three:	TRANSPORT AND INDUSTRY	37
Chapter Four:	TWO WORLD WARS	57
Chapter Five:	EDALE SCHOOL	65
Chapter Six:	CHURCH AND CHAPEL	79
Chapter Seven:	RECREATION	87
Chapter Eight:	CLUBS AND SOCIETIES	107
Chapter Nine:	SPORTS	121
Chapter Ten:	NATURAL HISTORY	129
Chapter Eleven:	THE NATIONAL TRUST	131
Chapter Twelve:	EDALE FAMILIES	137
	Subscribers	158

Acknowledgements

The Edale Society wishes to record its thanks to the following for their work on this book. Whether carrying out research, collecting or supplying photographs and documents, or recording reminiscences, their combined contributions have made this book possible. We are indebted to those who have found the time to record the wealth of information and to put it into a readable form:

David Baird, Campie Barrows, Denise Thwaites Bee, Julia Belton, Ashlyn Bower, Mildred Bramwell, James Carrington, Jean and Alan Chapman, Margaret Connors, Roger and Penny Cooper, Bob Cottrill, Andrew Critchlow, Belinda Critchlow, Adrian Earp, Fairlie Elrington, John Gee, Val Gilbert, Margaret Grassby, Shelagh Gregory, R. Hadfield, Milly Heardman, Robert Helliwell, David Howe, Leslie and Ella Inskip, Rob and Caroline Jackson, Tony Jackson, Carol Jamieson, Sheila McHale, Norah McKeon, Gordon Miller, Revd Adrian Murray-Leslie, John Nield, Brenda Oakes, Judy and Phil Oldroyd, Sandra Pillans, Jean Rodwell, Jenny Rodwell, Tom Rowbottom, Muriel Shirt, Geoff and Coral Sims, Derek, Margaret and Gwen Sowerby, Julia Thompson, Steve Trotter, Amy Tym, Maud Tym, Clive Wetherall, Margaret Wrenn, Dora Yates.

The Shirt family haymaking at Lee Farm, Upper Booth, probably around the early 1900s.

Introduction

A wild and isolated valley, a place of industrial hardship, a tourist mecca. All these describe Edale over the past 150 years. Situated in the heart of the Peak National Park, Edale has had to adapt to major changes in its social and economic structure over a relatively short period of time. It is remarkable that it still has so many tangible links to its past. The tapestry that is the Edale Valley is the result of centuries of agricultural activity that have shaped the landscape we see today. The Industrial Revolution did not pass us by and the drovers and the mill and railway workers all left an indelible print on this beautiful valley. Now Edale struggles to cope with ever-increasing numbers of walkers who seek the solitude provided by the high moors above the valley. In this age of mobility and advancing technology it is perhaps a good time to reflect on how those who lived in isolated communities like Edale were able to adapt and become self reliant, often in harsh and difficult conditions. As we look forward to another century of change we can, through these pages, look back on some of the events that have taken place over the past century and see many of the diverse elements that have contributed to making this valley such a unique place.

The Edale Valley from Ringing Roger.

Mam Tor and the Iron-Age fort with Skinner's Hall in the foreground.

Edale Cross, an ancient monument marking an ecclesiastical boundary from medieval times.

Chapter One

EARLY EDALE

The name Edale is probably derived from a combination of Old English and Norse. In Old English 'ea' is water and 'dôel' means meadow, and the Norse 'dalr' also means meadow. This can therefore be translated as water-meadow or island meadow. Some sources propose it could even be an island valley. Suggestions as to how this name came to be applied are subjective. One school of thought proposes that an area between the River Noe and the Grinds Brook is the island, while a more favoured suggestion is that the valley with its water-meadows is an island surrounded, not by water, but high moorland.

Prehistory

Edale has varied in size and importance since the first records. The great site of Mam Tor Iron-Age settlement dominates the skyline. These settlers left a dramatic legacy and record of their lives here. But there is evidence of even earlier Edalians.

In prehistoric times, before writing had come into existence, previous generations wandered the valley and hilltops of Edale. They left evidence of their lives on the landscape – the standing stones and stone circles provide our earliest local records of megalithic peoples, with trading and other routes written on our hills as early paths and trackways. The Portway running along Rushop Edge over Lord's Seat, then on to the northern side of Mam Tor, and a second ancient track on Mam Tor itself, are evidence of prehistoric routes. These routes were perhaps as well used then as they are now, when the parascenders and hang-gliders, walkers and ramblers, have taken the place of those early people who sought a safe and direct ridgeway above the dangerous valley where wolves and bears roamed.

Archaeological surveys have been few and far between, but Thomas Bateman, a noted archaeologist, wrote in 1848 that one of the barrows on Mam Tor had been opened and 'a brass celt and some fragment of an unbaked urn were found.' Little has been discovered of earlier times, but it is thought that people have roamed and settled here since the Ice Age, which helped to form and shape the valley.

Even before that, in c.12,000BC (middle Stone Age or early Mesolithic period), hunter-gatherers could well have wandered as far as Edale. There is evidence of them at Star Carr in North Yorkshire and at Poulton le Fyde in Lancashire, and these peoples would have hunted across wide areas in a landscape very different from the one we know today, with dense forests and large areas of lagoon and lake. Britain was still joined at that time to the rest of Europe by a narrow land bridge, which was not submerged until about 6,300BC (and not rejoined until the latter part of the twentieth century AD). However, about 11,000 years ago the local landscape was becoming more recognisable – meadowsweet and dock, willow, birch, hazel and pine, oak, elm and ash seed have been identified along with large areas of sphagnum moss.

From 4,000BC people in this part of the world stopped travelling and following food chains. They abandoned their nomadic existence and began to settle and farm. The climate was mainly clement with warm summers and mild winters – rather like the weather of the twenty-first century. Situated near the highest point of Mam Tor (517 metres), two Bronze-Age round barrows were excavated, first by Thomas Bateman and later during five successive digs in the 1960s when a late-Bronze-Age socketed axe was discovered.

Mam Tor, Iron-Age Fort Settlement

In 1159BC a huge volcano called Hekla erupted near the coast of Iceland. There is evidence that a layer of volcanic ash spread over much of Northern Europe, and it has been suggested that this hastened the shift to permanent settlements. Certainly by 1,000BC the climate was again changing to create a cooler, wetter environment in which huge areas of blanket bog appeared in upland regions and restricted farming areas. Around this time palisades and ditches were dug to surround and possibly protect the Iron-Age hill-fort settlements like Mam Tor. These were on trading routes and were market centres as well as settlements capable of defence.

Mam Tor Iron-Age hill-fort settlement is one of the biggest in the country, covering an area of approximately 17 acres. The interior covers 12 acres and there are clear indications of hut platforms cut into the internal slopes on both the sheltered eastern and more exposed western sides. It must have housed many people in the early part of the first millennium BC. Yet despite its impressive size and position no full archaeological surveys were undertaken until the 1960s. In 1950 a rim shard of coarse dark-grey ware was picked up on Mam Tor by a Mrs C. Guido and is now in the Sheffield Museum. Later, a complete Iron-Age pot dated 1,000–800BC, three inches high and coloured light brown with dark-grey tones, was found on Back Tor (now also in the museum), linking present Edalian pot makers with an ancient past.

Between 1965 and 1969 five excavations were undertaken by staff and students of the University of Manchester. At this time a proton magnetometer survey uncovered charcoal, pottery, circular hearths of stone slabs and potsherds. It appeared to have been a fairly permanent dwelling. There was a palisade, earth rampart and huts, but very little evidence of post holes. Perhaps they used the same drystone walling techniques that we see everywhere today on the hillsides and for sheep pens, or perhaps the walls were of turf.

Little has survived of the dwellings themselves. The walls of the homes might have been of turf or drystone walls or, as in other parts of the country, of wattle and daub – the upright timbers interwoven with coppiced wood (hazel, oak, ash or willow) covered with a weatherproof layer of daub (clay, soil, straw and animal manure). The huts were about 13 feet in diameter with a narrow doorway scarcely two feet wide. In here there would have been smoked meat above the fire to sustain the settlers through long winters. However, the acid soil has eaten up most evidence with only a few scraps of unidentifiable bone remaining for the students to find. Charcoal from two of the huts has produced carbon dates from the twelfth century BC.

The rampart was found to be of simple dump construction with stone revetment and a stone-faced retaining wall. The ditch was flat bottomed and seven feet deep. A number of the hut sites were excavated and consisted of semi-circular gulleys and post holes set in a levelled platform cut into the hillside. The people who lived here were one of many Celtic tribal groups, inhabiting an area big enough to defend a small tribal family and their stock, if necessary.

These first settled Edalians farmed some of the higher land around Mam Tor and drank from the spring that still exists there. They wore woollen clothing from the sheep they kept for milk, wool and meat. Basic cooking pots of hand-shaped local clay (like the one found on Back Tor) were hung over the fire where meat would be cooked or smoked. An upright weaving loom would have been used to make woollen garments, often brightly coloured with natural dyes and sometimes with striped or checked patterns.

The Romans and After

Would these people look so different to modern eyes? To the Romans they seemed very strange. When they arrived and settled nearby at the Navio fort at Brough and the mining settlement in Castleton their writers, like Strabo, recorded how different these clothes were to the plain tunics and togas worn by the Romans. Close-fitting trousers (braccae) held up with a belt, a tunic and a cloak formed the everyday wardrobe of both men and women. Their hair was long, sometimes plaited, and most men grew beards and/or long moustaches.

Caesar described Britain as a land of small farms. Certainly, farming and growing crops must have been part of daily life in the Mam Tor settlement. People have much in common the whole world over at different times and in different cultures – one thing we seem to have learned is the need for an aid to relaxation. When the Romans arrived they found a local beer produced in Britain, made, explains Pliny, by fermenting grain flavoured with local plants like nettle, the surface foam (yeasts) being used also in bread making.

There were four dates for festivals at this time:

Beltane   *May 1st*
Lugnasad   *August 1st*
Samhain   *November 1st*
Imbolc   *February 1st*

All the dates, it is believed, were tied in with the agricultural calendar, although Samhain, or Hallowe'en, was also the time when spirits could pass between the worlds. This date has again become a festive time in the village when children party and, as in other cultures, 'trick or treat' villagers.

The Brigantes fought fiercely against the Romans in the North East, but were defeated. It can only be imagined that the incomers soon became part of the Hope Valley, settling and raising families in Castleton, Hope and possibly Edale, although evidence of dwellings is sparse for this period as by this time Mam Tor was no longer inhabited.

By the seventh century AD the Romano British people were still here, a part of the local scene. The Roman road over the Snake remained the only route in that direction until the 1820s. But Derbyshire was in a state of flux, divided between the Danes and the Saxons. South Derbyshire (Danes) was in the kingdom of Elmut, and North Derbyshire (Saxons) that of Mercia, with Edale somehow sitting in the middle between the two kingdoms. In 942AD the Treaty of Dove, a peaceful name, settled the border down the Hope Valley!

Edale in the Middle Ages

Edale had a few families herding cattle at this time (there is no record of sheep). It was by now part of

EARLY EDALE

the Saxon Royal Borough with rents of £30 plus five carts of lead for the large area of Hope, Bakewell and Ashford. Before 1066, the 'bailiwicks' of Edale and Aston had land for ten ploughs. But things changed.

Records in the Domesday Book and of life in Edale show a decrease in farming rents – change is constant. By 1086 there was land for six ploughs only in Edale and Aston, and our name was recorded in the Domesday Book. Subsequent changes and permutations of name are as follows:

Aidele	1086
Heydale	1251
Eydale	1275
Eydal	1285
Edall	1550
Edale	1732

Edale stands on Grinds Brook and Grindsbrook Booth was first mentioned in 1342, named after the stream on which it stands, then known as Grim's Brook. Ollerbrook Booth (1561) is similarly named after the stream 'Alder Brook'.

In the Domesday Book, Edale is recorded as part of the 'Berewick' of Hope in the Royal Forest of the Peak. In Hope Church the thirteenth-century tombstones of forest officials can be seen – they were rather like Peak Park officers of today – with an engraved hatchet, the symbol of their office. There are records of members of the Eyre family being employed and of the animals they killed. In 1160 and 1161 wolf keepers were recorded and wolf traps were set up twice a year. In the thirteenth century a 'colt was strangled by a wolf' in Edale.

Deer roamed the valley (many dying in the terrible snowstorms of 1635) until 1674 when they were rounded up and killed or used for ploughing and livestock. Before that time, in the sixteenth century, temporary shelters for summer pasturing of beasts – both sheep and cattle – were established in 'booths'.

Hope and Castleton were thriving centres as the building of Peveril Castle (Norman) shows, linking it to the other Norman castles in Bolsover and Nottingham. In fact, with its caves, castle and mines, Castleton was by the twelfth century being described as one of the four wonders of England.

Travellers have found Mam Tor an endless source of fascination. Both Celia Fiennes and Daniel Defoe 1660–1731 (of *Robinson Crusoe* fame) visited and, along with the Peak Cavern (now Devil's Arse) in Castleton, listed it among the 'Seven Wonders of Derbyshire'. Mam Tor was the fifth wonder out of seven from the 'Seven Wonders of the Peak':

> *... unlike in stature and in substance this*
> *To the south east is a great precipice*
> *Not of firm rock, like the rest here that shroud*
> *Their loving summits in a dewy cloud:*
> *But of a shaley earth, that from the crown*
> *With a continued motion mould'ring down,*
> *Spawns a less hill of looser mould below,*
> *Which will in time tall as the mother grow,*
> *And must perpetuate the wonder so.*
> *Which wonder is that though this hill never cease*
> *To waste itself, it suffers no decrease...*

Mam Tor means 'Mother Rock', and Defoe's explanation is that the constant crumbling produced smaller mountains beneath. Fiennes, the travel writer, wrote in her book, *The Journeys of Celia Fiennes*, of the face on the Castleton side, '... it is all broken that it looks just in resemblance as a great Hayricke that cuts down on one side.'

Wainwright, in the *Pennine Way Companion* of 1965, notes:

> *Neither Kirk Yetholm nor Edale have any features that make them obvious choices as termini: both are small villages without any outstanding characteristics or geographical highlights or historical importance...*

Lambing time in Edale in the late 1800s.

Edale Shepherds' Society in the late 1800s.

Chapter Two

FARMS AND FARMING

The history of farming in Edale goes back to prehistoric times, when our ancestors began to cultivate crops and rear animals in order to survive the long winters. At the time of writing, farming is still one of the most important industries in the valley.

An article written in 1917 by C.B. Fawcett endorses the idea that the name Edale means island. He notes that the widest part of the Edale Valley from crest to crest is three miles, but he goes on to add 'the width of the habitable portion nowhere exceeds one mile, and averages little more than half that distance.' Fawcett adds that the moors to the north-west of the valley 'exceed an altitude of 2,000 feet for a length of three miles.' This makes the depth of the valley around 1,000 feet. In this sense, Edale is an island, or oasis, set in the moorlands of the High Peak.

LOCAL CONDITIONS

The narrowness and depth of the valley means that the valley sides are extremely steep. The soil is thin and in places there are rock outcrops, known as tors. Small streams cut into the sides of the valley. The streams, the most notable of which are Grinds Brook and Crowden Brook, run into the River Noe. These gullies, or cloughs, created by these streams vary in depth – some tend to be small ravines while others are relatively shallow, wet-weather streams.

Glacial melt water produced the main valley. The soft shales and clay were easily washed away, resulting in the development of a U-shaped valley. The fertile lower slopes developed as a result of weathering and by the wash and creep of the material from the steep slopes. Into the bottom of this the River Noe continues to cut a groove.

Fawcett's report of 1917 gives a detailed description of the valley. The climatic conditions are illustrated with figures recorded by the Derwent Valley Water Board from rain gauges at Upper Booth and Dale Head (a total of nine rain gauges were established by the Water Board). Between 1906 and 1914 the average rainfalls for these two sites were 52.09 inches (1323.09 mm) and 48.07 inches (1220.98 mm) per annum. The climate also varied between the east and west ends of the valley. During the period 1940–55, records show that Jacob's Ladder at Edale Head received 11.63 inches (26.7 per cent) per annum more than Edale End, the lowest and driest point in the valley where the monthly averages for all 12 months were lower than those of any of the other gauges.

Improved and cultivated ground is found along the lower slopes, with farms and houses concentrated along the northern side of the river in order to benefit from the longer hours of sunshine received compared to the southern side of the valley. This is illustrated by a name given to a section of the valley side below Mam Tor, known as 'Cold Side'. In winter the sun does not get high enough above the ridge that stretches from Losehill to Mam Tor and along Rushup Edge to have any lasting effect on the southern side of the valley. The result is that frosts can last many days in winter along the north-facing slope.

Soils along the valley floor have naturally poor drainage and tend to be heavy and inherently low in fertility. This is exacerbated by the high rainfall of the area, which not only causes leaching of nutrients, but also continues to wash soil down the slopes. Shale outcrops are common, particularly along the side of the River Noe, and are the main reason for the designation of the upper reaches of the River Noe as a Site of Special Scientific Interest (SSSI). Landslips are another feature of the valley, again resulting from the unstable rock strata, and represent another factor that makes the ground unsuitable for cultivation. The high moors to the north and west are covered in blanket bog with peat varying between two and three metres in depth. It is known that peat has been cut around Edale since medieval times.

The weather, soil type and topography have a major influence on the type of farming carried out in Edale, with livestock farming dominating the valley throughout its history.

THE EARLY FARMERS

Although there is evidence of man's presence in Edale during the Neolithic period, the first written evidence of farming of various sorts materialises in the Domesday Book. Under the Saxons, Edale was part of the Royal Manor of Hope. The Domesday record shows it as a berewick, or outlying area of the manor:

11

Littlewood Cottage, Barber Booth, now demolished, is thought to have been one of the oldest houses in Edale. An Anglo-Saxon cruck barn is situated nearby.

In Hope, with the outliers Aidele [Edale], Estune [Aston], Scetune [Shatton], half of Offertune [Offerton], Tidesuuelle [Tideswell], Stoche [Stoke] Muchedesuuelle [Muchedeswell], King Edward had 10c of land taxable. Land for 10 ploughs.

Now 30 villagers and 4 smallholders have 6 ploughs. A priest and a church, to which belongs 1c of land.

1 mill, 5s 4d; meadow 30 acres; woodland pasture in places 4 leagues and 2 furlongs long and 2 leagues wide.

Before 1066 these manors paid £30, 5 ½ sesters of honey and 5 wagon-loads of 50 lead sheets: now they pay £10. 6s.

William Peveril has charge.

[c = caracute – unit of land measurement]

It is not possible to deduce from this how many farms there were in the Vale of Edale as there are no separate details for each berewick. Prior to the Domesday survey woodland had started to be cleared in the valley, creating pasturage for cattle.

In 1068 William Peveril gave lands in Edale to the monks at Spitalfields Hospital, Castleton, for 'the grazing of 8 beasts and pannagel and a garden for the growth of herbs for medicinal purposes.' The monks would have left someone to look after their interests in Edale. There would have been a need for a byre or shelter for the stock and a requirement for protection against wolves, which were present in the area into the sixteenth century. At this time the first enclosures may have been established to aid livestock keeping, and huts built for the use of the stock keepers. These early stock keepers would have been more likely to make use of the valley floor and lower slopes as these would have been of better quality than those higher up.

Monastic pasturage developed into a system of ranching whereby cattle and horses were reared for sale along with sheep. The latter supplied valuable meat, fat and fleeces. The system would have been self-sufficient but the climate would have limited the amount of arable land. The number of ploughs noted in the Domesday survey indicates that some plough land probably existed, and there is early evidence of a mill.

During the reign of King John, use of the valley became more formalised. His second wife, Isabella of Angouleme, bred horses here and established the booths or vaccaries (from the Latin 'vacca' for cow) between 1199–1216. Early records show that in 1391/92 the sum of £6.10s.8d. was received for winter herbage in Edale, Castleton and other nearby villages.

By the early-fourteenth century these pastures were of some importance, as indicated by the following Crown Rents for the Royal Forest of the Peak between 1339 and 1413:

John and Ric Barber, for a booth in Heydall [no amount given]
John Barber Thomas Hall and Elis Smith for a booth in Heydall £9 13s 4d
Thos. Pursglove, for a booth in Heydall £9 0s 0d
Rob. Barber Thos Hall and Rich Howe for a booth in Heydall £9 6s 8d
Thos. Smith for a booth in Heydall £8 15s 0d

FARMS AND FARMING

These are not annual rents. If the figures shown are equated to contemporary values the rents would be considerable. They indicate that these were substantial holdings with enclosures, with at least one house each as well as buildings.

Tithes feature strongly in Edale's farming history. A dispute between the Cistercian monks from the Abbey of Vale Royal near Nantwich and the monks from Lenton Abbey, Nottinghamshire, arose over the question of who should receive the tithes from these lands. In 1328 the Abbott of the Abbey of Vale Royal petitioned the Queen:

> ... to the most honourable lady our Lady Queen Isabel... that they should deliver the tithes of Eydale which is in the parish of Chastelton in the Peak, whereof he has always been seised...

'Tithe of cattle of the said Queen, bred and fed in Eydale' is also mentioned in the petition.

The Abbot of Vale Royal was also rector of the church of Castleton, but it was not until then that the Bishop of Chester granted the tithes to the rectory of Castleton, which were later leased out by one Richard Torr in 1688.

The Royal Hunting Forest

Edale was part of the Forest of the Peak (Foresta de Pecco) – a royal hunting forest established by the Normans. The forest was chiefly open country, divided into three wards – Hopedale, Longdedale and Campana (or Champayne, from which is derived the name of Champion). It was administered by the Duchy of Lancaster for the King. Sir Richard Vernon was steward of the Peak until 1445. He lived at Haddon Hall and was considered a despot. He leased pastures from the Duchy in the 1470s and 1480s to the south of Edale. His grandson, Sir Henry Vernon, leased a vaccary in Edale. Forest rules were known to be hard and penalties severe if they were broken. An example of forest law shows that in 1398 'John de Sale, boothman of Edale was presented for receiving 2 marks for the sale of wood'. This suggests that he was presented at court for selling wood illegally and would presumably have received some penalty.

By the late-fifteenth century the forest was in decline and parts were being sold off. At this time the booths were in the hands of freeholders and freed from forest rules. The lands in the Royal Forest of the Peak were known to be used for grazing beasts (cattle, sheep and horses), for deer and for turbary (peat and turf cutting). Rushoop (Rushup) fell into this latter category. Here the foresters were allowed to take and to sell peat and turf. To the north of the valley Peat Moor was for common turbary usage. It is estimated that this peat-cutting area was probably one of the biggest in Derbyshire and may have been used for over 1,000 years.

In about 1600, Anthony Bradshaw wrote, with regard to the 'Fforestade Alto Pecco': 'This fforest of Longdendale whereof therle of Shr [the Earl of Shrewsbury] ys the fforester: and the fforest of Ashopp and Edail, the said Earle being Ranger.' It is apparent from this that Edale and the Forest of the Peak was a very important area of the High Peak. This is also borne out by the presence of Peveril Castle at Castleton. A map of the forest made c.1581–90 shows Edale and the woodlands as 'The Queenes Majestys farms... divided into five vaccaries.'

Documentation is available from the early 1600s to show that land was changing hands:

> The 6th Earl of Shrewsbury [George Talbot, d.1590] had leased much of the eastern richer part of the valley but at some time this had become ownership for... in 1625 the Shrewsbury Estate arranged the sale for £590 to one Stephen Bright [1583–1642] of 'A vaccary called Lady Booth alias Tunstead Leighs or Nether Booth – also a Mill, a bull and kine'.

In 1653 James Bright purchased 'closes and land at Over Nether Backtor for £2,500'. Other Shrewsbury land passed to the Dukes of Newcastle and then to the Dukes of Devonshire, who owned it into the 1900s. The Lord Scarsdale of Sutton Scarsdale also acquired land in 1700. At Ollerbrook there is evidence of middlemen selling land to the Hall family in the 1620s.

In around 1631 Ralph Cresswell (sometimes spelt Creswell) came into Edale from Malcoff in Chapel-en-le-Frith. He and one Giles Barber took land in Edale when it was disafforested. The original grant was from the Trustees of the Corporation of London. The Corporation had lent Charles I a large sum of money in return for a grant of Crown lands. It was these trustees that sold land in Edale to Ralph Cresswell and Giles Barber. Cresswell's share was known as Crowden-le-Booth, now called Upper Booth, while Barber purchased lands at Whitemorelea Booth.

Despite the sales, the Crown continued to charge some rents for these freehold properties. These were fee farm rents, a perpetual rent of at least a quarter of the value of the land. These rents could be sold off by the Crown to individuals who in turn could sell them on. There is evidence that some of these rents were still being paid to the Crown in the 1700s on property at Barber Booth. Even later, legal papers dated 1922 detailed a mortgage between one Samuel Thornely and several of his tenants and listed the amount due as 'fee farm rents' as follows:

Part of Field Head	£9.0s.
Cote Farm (Smiths Cottage)	£1.4s.
Rowlands Farm (formerly called Littlewood Farm)	2s.2d.
Small Clough	12s.2d.

THE BOOK OF EDALE

Shearing and wrapping fleeces in the 1920s.

FARMS AND FARMING

Littlewood Cottage   3s.
Consecration money payable to the Incumbent of Edale
    Church from Rowlands Farm
                        6s.8d.
Total   £1.11s.7d.

The population of Edale is known to have grown rapidly in the early 1600s. The Hearth Tax of 1670 indicates that there were 230 souls. By the middle of the eighteenth century there was prosperity as outlying farms and barns were established. These were first recorded on the Hope parish map of 1808 and the tithe map of 1839.

Sheep Farming in Edale

Early in the eighteenth century, sheep numbers were noted to be so high in the tithe records that the moors were showing noticeable overgrazing. For sheep there were inventory days when counts would take place. These were 12–14 June (Lamb Day) and 9–10 July (Wool Day, the day when woolled sheep were counted). Sheep were listed in the inventory as 'In', 'Out' or 'Up'. That is, folded, unfolded or for tithe respectively. Tithes were payable in kind until 1747 when some large flock owners came to an arrangement whereby tithes were commuted to 1s. (5p) for every ten sheep for wool, and 3½d. (2p) per lamb.

In addition, tithe payments were due from each booth for small items and for services rendered to each other such as winter folding, washing and shearing. In the early-eighteenth century there were some 45 flock owners paying tithes. Tithes were payable on all livestock and crops. It seems that the people of Edale had been in dispute with Richard Torr, lessee of the tithes, over their payment in 1660, claiming that they had been discharged of all tithe payments except for a payment of 40 shillings. Judgement was cast in favour of Torr for wool and lamb, but agreement in favour of the people of Edale for hay and corn was given.

The tithe maps show owners and occupiers of land and buildings. On the south side holdings had a

Whitefaced Woodland sheep, once common in Edale, at Ladybooth Hall Farm in Nether Booth.

nucleus of in-bye land around the farm that extended upwards to the rough grazings. A similar situation prevailed on the north side with the exception of Upper and Grindsbrook Booths. In this case it seems that the moorland had shared ownership, possibly reflecting traditional grazing and peat-cutting rights.

The average size of flock was 53 sheep, with only ten sheep keepers having more than 100 head. Lamb crops were very moderate with an average of 0.32 lambs per sheep. However, it must be considered that not all adult sheep would be expected to lamb. A young ewe would have had her first lamb at two or three years of age, while wethers (castrated males) would be kept until a similar age before slaughter. No reference is made to tithes due on other livestock such as cattle, horses or pigs.

In the early-nineteenth century farm help was sought at the annual Hiring Fairs, probably at Hope or Castleton. The *Derby Mercury* of 23 September 1813 printed an apology dated 17 September of the same year from one William Shirt. The apology was to 'Mr Champion for having left his employ, having been convicted and served one month.' A one-month sentence was the standard penalty for leaving the employment of a master within the year of employment.

Barns and Walls

It was at the beginning of the nineteenth century that a large number of field barns were built throughout the valley. Most holdings had one field barn if some land was not adjacent to the holding. Many of these barns are still in existence, but some have fallen into disrepair. Their purpose was for the storage of winter feed (hay) for livestock, the livestock in turn supplying not only meat, milk and wool, but also manure to be used as a source of fertilizer. Barns often incorporated cow byres, indicating that cattle were an important part of farming in the valley. During the nineteenth century it is known that cattle grazed the higher ground while the valley meadows were used for haymaking.

Sheep wash around the late 1940s.

Above: *Sheep washing, possibly in Grindsbrook, between the wars. John Shirt is in the foreground. It was popular to wear the Homburg hat with the band removed and the hollow pushed out at the top.*

Right: *Horse and sled being used to carry winter feed for sheep, c.1940s.*

Shearing sheep, c.1920.

FARMS AND FARMING

To aid sheep keeping on the moorland, sheepfolds were built, usually on the boundary of the moorland and the enclosed ground. These would be used for sorting sheep as they were gathered off the moors. The remains of these folds are still visible, for example in Crowden Clough, close to the summit of Jacob's Ladder, Peat Moor and Ladybrook, and are often marked on the earlier Ordnance Survey maps of the valley. Sheepfolds were also built in conjunction with sheep washes. These can be found at various points in the valley where streams or the river could be easily dammed. Sheep were then washed in the clean water to remove impurities from the fleece before shearing. This practice continued into the twentieth century. Remains of sheep washes can be found in Jagger's Clough, Grindsbrook and Crowden Clough.

On the exposed higher ground can be found the remains of sheep lees. These were short runs of drystone wall built against the prevailing wind, their purpose being to provide shelter for sheep during bad weather. Most of these are on the southern side of the valley below the summit of Rushup Edge. One of these is built in the shape of a 'Y', offering some protection against the weather regardless of wind direction.

Field Names

The field system in existence at the time of writing is very similar to that shown on the 1840 tithe map and on surveys carried out in seventeenth and eighteenth centuries. Indications are that by the early 1600s the current field system was already established. Consequently, Edale was not affected to any great extent by the Enclosure Acts of the early-nineteenth century. Meadows were generally found near streams, with the pastures running up the slopes from the meadows. Long, thin fields of two to four acres were ideal for pasturing and for rotating stock, while fields on the steeper valley sides are larger. These are known as 'outpastures' and 'intakes'. On the south side, the intakes tended to get larger, which may reflect the poor quality growth of grass on this side of the valley.

Many fields were given names and this has proved useful in tracing past land use or ownership. A field at the foot of Rushup Edge is known as the Poor Piece because the proceeds from its use were for the benefit of the parish poor. A similar field to the west of Highfield benefited Castleton School. Thisley is a common name for pastures, suggesting that they may have grown good thistles, while Gorsey Side suggests that gorse grew rather well. Hagg Lee may get its name from the old practice of cutting holly for winter feed. Newlands, New Field or Newground implies that this was a new field that had been taken in and improved from the moorland. Rye Flatt is found at Ollerbrook and implies that this cereal may once have been grown there.

It seems that the car park and tips at Barber Booth are situated on the site of a field called Kiln Piece, indicating the presence of limekilns. 'Pingle' features widely in the field names of the valley. This merely indicates that the field is irregular in shape. Ox Pasture, Cow Hey, Milking Steads and Horse Pasture obviously relate to the grazing of livestock, while Donkey Shed Field is self-explanatory, and this does indicate that these animals were kept in the valley. At Grindslow there are fields called Doctor's and Parson's Piece. These may have been for grazing the said gentlemen's horses, or may have been let to provide an income. There is also a Church Piece at Barber Booth, which may have been originally endowed to the church, or the produce from that field sold for the benefit of the church. Prison Field at Crookstone may have been named as such because prisoners built the walls around it, or had a camp there.

Field boundaries in the valley are a mixture of hedgerows and drystone walls. Hedges can be found on the lower slopes, with the exception of an area around Ollerbrook where walls reach almost down to the river. Drystone walls were often built by gangs of men, or prisoners of the Napoleonic Wars. The following letter written in 1784 refers to walling at Edale Head, and also sheds some light on important social issues of the time:

Mr Fox
I am much obliged to you for your letter and am willing to pay Thos. Cooper four shillings a week to take care of Edale Head and wall the gaps, and also one shilling and fourpence a rood for new walls to be 74 inches high and eight yards to the rood. He is welcome to live in the house rent free as he ought to be there day and night, only to come two nights a week to get his wife with child. As to pulling down the wall I give but 2d a rood. But if he requires it James and Low shall pull it down a day.

The money I will leave in your hands to pay him every week if he chooses it.

I cannot travel on Sunday Evening after divine service therefore you will let me see you on Tuesday.

James shall meet Thomas Cooper on Monday Morning with two tups.
I am
Your friend

B Bower*

Stockport
5th November 1784

[*The name of Buckley Bower appears on Poor Law assessment records for Crowden-lee-Booth 1785]

Land and Cultivation

The main periods of land cultivation for arable are likely to have been between 1772 and 1781, and from 1825 until 1835, when the climate was warmer and

Jim Carrington passes Church Cottage, c.1930.

Jack Tym mowing in 1893.

FARMS AND FARMING

Lee Farm, Upper Booth, with water trough in foreground.

wetter and gave a better growing season. Oats were the main cereal crop and these were used for both animal and human feed, oat bread and oat cakes being a staple food at this time.

From 1842–47, 20 per cent of the land was cultivated, probably on a rotational basis, taking advantage of relatively new husbandry techniques. Root crops were grown for winter fodder. Threshing barns can still be found around the valley, and there are records of mills at Nether Booth and also on the site of the existing Edale Mill building, adding further evidence that corn has been grown in Edale.

Much of the pasture land was 'ridge and furrow', some of it possibly dating to medieval times. This is still in evidence at Highfield Farm, Upper Booth, and below Broadlee Bank. Other areas that were likely to have once been ridge and furrow have been cultivated and ploughed out along with other archaeological features, particularly during the 'WarAg' years of the Second World War.

Maps of 1825 and 1847 (Edale's tithe map and the Hope parish map respectively) show larger areas of moorland than can be seen at the time of writing. The maps show cairns on moors to the north of the valley. It is thought that the marked divisions of grazing rights refer to the booth boundaries and to areas of ownership, but these have since fallen out of use.

The Effects of the Railway

By the mid-1800s vacant properties were noted and, despite the coming of the railway, there began a decline in the number of holdings that has continued to the time of writing.

An insight into the value of live and dead stock at the beginning of the twentieth century is illustrated by the ledger accounts for the sale of the property of Mrs Grace Elliott, thought to have taken place at Dale Head, on 30 September 1901. This was a complete dispersal sale. It included small tools such as forks (four were sold to 'Eyre' for 6d.), spades (sold to 'Tym' for 6d.), scythes (two sold to 'Cooper' for 1s.), and a hay knife (also sold to 'Cooper', for 2s.3d.). Harnesses and saddles were sold, a pair of hames were sold to J. Thorpe for 8s., while a 'Sunday Harness' was sold to 'Eyre' for 1s. 'Rowbottom' bought the chaff-cutter for 1s. A heavy cart was sold to 'Elliott' for £5. Livestock sales included sheep of all ages. Nine ewes with lambs sold for 17s. to 'Burdekin'; a total of £7.13s.6d. Wethers sold for 18s. each, to 'Lindley', while one tup sold to 'J Thorpe' for £1.18s. Some 'Scotts' ewes were also included in the sale, selling for 23s. per head. From the brief detail given for the cattle, they would appear to have been shorthorn types. Roan calves sold at £3.7s.6d. to 'Champion', a white heifer sold for £6.2s.6d. to 'Helliwell', and a cow in milk sold to 'Bradley' for £8.5s. A brown mare fetched nine guineas and its foal seven guineas, both sold to 'Cooper'. A 'Cur dog' sold to 'A Robinson' for £1.15s. Mrs Elliott grew corn, as a total of five corn stacks were sold to Messrs Needham, Shirt and Champion for various amounts up to £4.17s.6d. The total for the receipts for the sale were £289.10s.8d., while the auctioneers' costs amounted to £15.16s.6d.

At a time when technology was advancing in most other rural areas, there was little in the way of income in the valley to afford equipment. The main sales would have been livestock and wool, but was in competition with produce from more productive areas, and so was at a disadvantage. Kirkam in 1917 commented on the state of the land and the benefits that the railway brought to the valley as a whole. Surpluses could be transported and supplies obtained more easily, which meant less reliance on self-sufficiency. One of the main effects was the abandonment of peat cutting. This had to be carried out in early summer when the peat was left to dry and then carted off before the wet weather came, but this coincided with hay time and when the corn was ready for harvesting, thus creating a heavy workload. The railways brought coal into the valley at a price that could be afforded as an acceptable alternative to peat.

The railways also opened up markets, in particular for milk sales. The demand was there from the large urban areas of Sheffield and Manchester, now easily accessible. It seems, however, that there was greater allegiance to Sheffield as it cost $^1/_2$d. per gallon less to send milk there. The journey to Manchester is six miles further, hence the extra cost.

It was also possible to transport livestock into the valley. Cattle were brought on the train to graze the hills, notably the area called The Pieces on Broadlee Bank, during the summer months.

Growing cereals must have been a risky business in Edale. At the start of the twentieth century little wheat was grown as it could not be ripened satisfactorily, and there are stories of how, during the Second World War, the grain sprouted in the ears before it could be harvested. However, vegetables were grown and potatoes rivalled oats as the most common arable crop. Root crops continued to be grown for fodder,

The road to Edale.

Eva, John and Jim Shirt of Nether Booth, 1925.

FARMS AND FARMING

Above: *A. Wilson delivering corn in 1926.*

Right: *Sheep shearing at Lee House in the late 1930s.*

J.W. Shirt senr, Jim Thornley senr and Jack Elliott, with his tractor made from old car parts. Mr Shirt bought the first purpose-built tractor into the valley, a grey Ferguson, in the late 1940s.

THE BOOK OF EDALE

Above: *Geoff Critchlow, on the right, selling his Fordson tractor at Shaw Wood Farm in February 1963.*

Left: *James and Sarah Gee at Cotefield Farm.*

Below: *Haymaking at Ivy House Farm in 1949.*

FARMS AND FARMING

Above: *Haymaking in the Lea Barn fields with John Rowbottom, local helpers and John's father Arthur on the hay cart in the 1950s.*

Right: *Cedric Gilbert and Paul Wheeldon at Nether Booth with a calf. Milk churns await collection in the background.*

Below: *Cedric Gilbert above Gibraltar Bridge in Grindsbook Booth. A farmer and parish councillor, Cedric was also for many years the local milkman.*

John B. Shirt on his father's Ferguson tractor in 1955 – this was the first production tractor in Edale in the 1940s.

but it was noted in 1916 that there was a mere 20 acres of farmland under arable cropping. Winters were more severe at that time and the supply of winter fodder tended to restrict the numbers of stock kept. As the summer came, stock could be moved to the higher ground while winter fodder (hay) was made on the lower grasslands. Kirkham noted the importance of ground game and wild fruit as a supplement to the diet of the valley's inhabitants, but he concluded that the area's production was poor and could be improved considerably if large areas of the valley were put down to forestry.

Recent Changes

A further analysis of Edale was published by Fawcett in 1957. He noted numerous derelict farmsteads, sometimes used as barns, and the peculiar pattern of holdings on the southern side of the valley denoting the abandonment of farms and purchase by neighbours. A total of 31 farms were noted, 20 less than during the First World War. The oldest farmsteads, many of which date from the mid-sixteenth century and have rarely changed hands, are situated in the five booths on the gentler northern slopes. Upper Booth is an exception, for only one of its five original farms remains.

In the upper part of the valley, tumbledown farm buildings and changes of farm ownership were noted as being more common. Many reasons, including isolation (electricity did not reach Upper Booth until the late 1950s), the rise in standards of farming and the difficulty of obtaining moorland grazing for sheep, contributed to the decline. Moor-grazing rights were regulated by the gate system, whereby one gate was the right to graze one sheep on the moor during one year. Formerly each holding had its share of gates but these had gradually been acquired by the older families and outsiders as farms changed ownership.

In 1957 it was noted that regularly employed labourers were few. Most farmers had a labour shortage, but their demands were more seasonal than permanent, especially on the small farms which suffered from the lack of haymaking machinery available that was cheap enough to justify the capital outlay. Partial mechanisation aggravated the labour problem by intensifying the seasonality of the demand and thus discouraging casual labourers.

At about this time there were 23 dairy herds in the valley. This was due to the proximity of large urban

Mary Wooley and John Rowbottom take a break from turning the hay, 1950s.

markets, road transport, the monthly milk cheque, and the consequent reduced importance of local fodder.

Farming in the Twenty-First Century

Farming, like most industries, has gone through a revolution. After the First World War there was a general depression in the state of agriculture. Farms were still labour-intensive and low in productivity. One of the most notable differences has to be the change from muscle power to machinery. In 2003 there are no working horses in the valley. Every farm has at least one tractor and associated machinery. All-terrain vehicles (ATVs) are considered essential for day-to-day work because they are quick and easy to manoeuvre.

The number of farms, and people engaged in farming activities, has continued to decline. Of a total of 15 working farms in the valley in December 2002, only two were dairy farms, the rest getting their farming income from sheep and beef production. Many of the valley farms are part of the North Peak Environmentally Sensitive Area. This government-run scheme is aimed at maintaining landscapes and encouraging wildlife, while putting the emphasis on low-input production. Its main effect in Edale has been to reduce the amount of sheep that graze on the Kinder plateau. The type of sheep kept has also changed. There are now more lowland types kept in the valley while the Woodland and Derbyshire Gritstone types of sheep have largely been replaced by the Swaledale with some Lonk and Suffolk blood.

At the start of the twenty-first century livestock production dominates the farming scene with very little ground under the plough. Land that is ploughed is used to grow forage crops. Sheep are the main enterprise on many of the farms producing lambs for sale as either stores, 'finished' or for breeding. There are some cattle, but only two dairy herds remain within the parish. Several farms have some beef cattle, but not in large numbers. Few holdings can rely on livestock production to provide sufficient income to maintain a family so there is a greater reliance on non-farming income in the form of diversified enterprises. These include camp-sites, bunk-house barns, camping barns, holiday cottages to let, a trekking centre and contract work. In other cases there may be a business running alongside the farm, or there may be a second income from working outside the valley, often brought in by a husband or wife going out to work. While returns from agricultural production are being depressed by globalisation and enlargement of the European Union, there is still

Shepherds' Society meeting around 1960, including, left to right: *Arthur Cotterill, Frank Wilson, Joe Townsend, Jim Thornley, Willie Shirt, ?, Stanley Sidebottom, ?, John Fox Shirt, Frank Critchlow, John Hadfield, ?, ?, ?, Eddie Hodgson* (black hair), *Ellis Hodgson, ?, Willis Bradbury, ?, ?, Harry Hallam. The tall man centre front is Jim Cooper.*

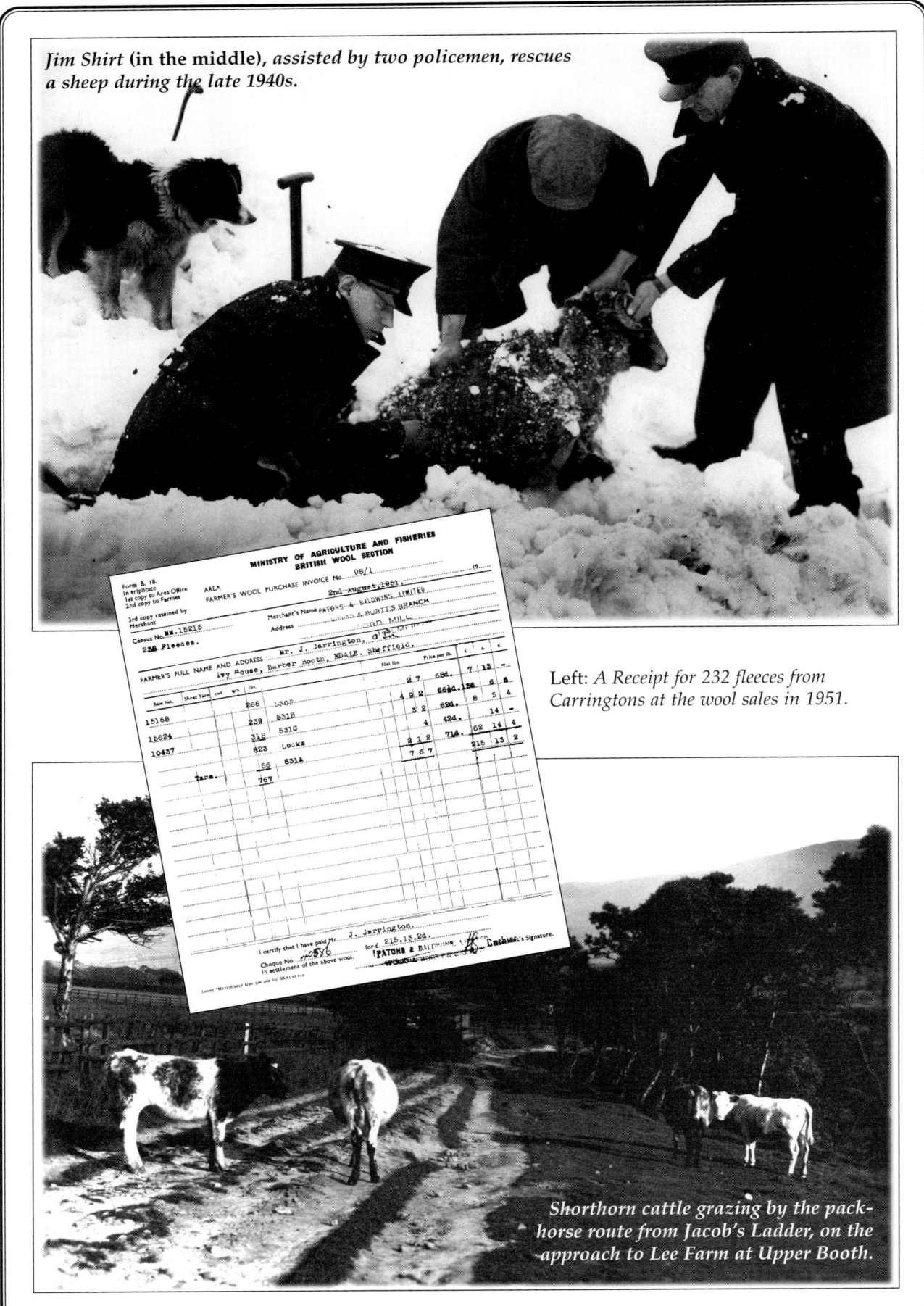

Jim Shirt (in the middle), *assisted by two policemen, rescues a sheep during the late 1940s.*

Left: *A Receipt for 232 fleeces from Carringtons at the wool sales in 1951.*

Shorthorn cattle grazing by the pack-horse route from Jacob's Ladder, on the approach to Lee Farm at Upper Booth.

FARMS AND FARMING

All-terrain vehicles are important pieces of machinery on farms in 2002.

a need to look after livestock which, in turn, are required to maintain the countryside in its familiar state. This calls for labour which, as was the case in 1957, is at a premium in the valley, particularly when it is possible to earn more money working in the cement works at Hope for fewer hours. Consequently, many farms are now run by one person, with hired help at certain busy times.

Edale Booths and Farms

The booths in Edale were originally established as 'vaccaries' or cattle farms in the early years of the thirteenth century. A map of 1585 shows the valley divided diagrammatically into five and early maps show cairns on the moors indicating boundaries of the various booths. In c.1830 the areas of each booth and some outlying farms were recorded as part of the tithe records. These are shown in the table overleaf. It seems that the boundaries of the booths have changed little over the years, giving a useful guide to the size of the individual booths. A packhorse route that linked the booths is still in evidence in various parts of the valley, but particularly as it enters the Vale of Edale from the west. The first map to show any real detail of Edale was that produced by Burdett in 1791.

Edale has evolved as five separate hamlets, or 'booths'. A booth was originally a herdsman's shelter for summer pasturing and the name is thought to come from the Germanic 'bude', meaning hut or shelter, similar to the Scottish word 'bothie'.

Within each booth there were at least four farmsteads with fields radiating outwards. In addition there were also field barns for fodder storage along with shippons for cattle wintering, stables, granaries and sheds for storage of implements and other equipment. The table overleaf offers some indication of the numbers of dwellings in each booth in 1839. Unfortunately, this survey did not include outlying properties. A feature of the valley at this time would have been small, rough dwellings known as cotes and hovels. These have been identified in the archaeological survey that was carried out in 1993, but it seems that not all were recorded. Rowland Cote (the site of the youth hostel at the time of writing) and Cote Fields Farm at Ollerbrook are examples, while there was also Cote Fields Farm at Upper Booth, the occupiers of which had grazing rights on Broadlee Bank. Edale's booths are:

Barber Booth
This was one of the original booths of Edale and dates from the time when Edale was part of the Royal Forest protected by the Castellon of Peveril Castle. The booth was originally known as Whitmorely Booth, although documents have referred to it both as Whitmore Lea Booth and Whitmore-le-Booth. It is believed that some of the houses present at the time of writing are built on the site of the original buildings, although evidence of a much older house can be seen incorporated into a barn. Whitmorley Booth was first referred to as Barber Booth in documents dating from the seventeenth century.

Grindsbrook Booth
Believed to have been occupied by foresters in the twelfth century, the original spelling is 'Grymsbroke', which appears frequently in old wills. It is thought by some to be associated with druid rites, with the prefix 'Gryms' referring to 'the evil one'. Druid amulets discovered in this area in the eighteenth century suggest that there may be some basis for this.

Ollerbrook Booth
Named due to its position on the Oller Brook as it flows down from Ashop Moor, farming pasture in Ollerbrook is referred to in a Barber family will of 1535. Another theory is that the name was once 'Alder Brook', so-called because of the alder trees growing along the brook. It has been suggested that the alder wood was used in the Lancashire clog industry.

Upper Booth
This was originally known as Crowdenley Booth, deriving its name from the Crowden Brook flowing down from Kinder Scout. Some documents refer to it as Crowden Lee Booth, Crowden-le-Booth or Crowdenly Booth. Documents show that the house at Crowdenley Booth was occupied by Ralph and Jane Barber during the reign of Queen Elizabeth I.

Nether Booth (Lady Booth)
Nether Booth was formerly known as Lower Booth, Lady Booth and prior to that Tunstydleyghe (Tunstead Leighes), a name derived from a farm in a clearing. It is still sometimes referred to as Lady Booth.

Upper Booth

Formerly Crowdenlea Booth (Crodenlie, Crodenley, Crowden-lee-Booth) and Over Booth, its original name is probably derived from a 'clearing in the valley of the crows'. Adjacent to Crowden Brook, the name of Upper Booth came into being after the road was made from Barber Booth to the south of the River Noe in the nineteenth century. There is evidence to suggest that there were five farms or smallholdings at Upper Booth.

The farmhouse which is in existence at Upper Booth Farm at the time of writing was built in 1830. Prior to this the holding was known as Shore Ground Farm. Crowden Lea (labelled as such on the 1842 tithe appointments), a private house at the time of writing, is one of the oldest houses in the valley and was once a farm of some importance.

Crowden Cottage was a small farm, while Arnfield Cottage was formerly Cote Fields Farm. Across the road from this was another farm known as Cote Farm, shown in the 1842 tithe appointment. This last farm was also a blacksmith's at some time. In addition there were two cottages within the bounds of what is the modern-day farmyard. The remains of two cotes have been identified in the fields. It is possible that more existed but it is difficult to distinguish between ruins of cotes and those of barns.

When Ralph Cresswell (Creswell) purchased 'Crowden-le-Booth' in 1651, there were substantial grazing rights for cattle and sheep on the hills. A descendant of his, Thomas Cresswell, converted part of a large barn into a school for the children in the immediate neighbourhood. This is the site of sheep pens at the time of writing. Robert Cresswell inherited the estate in 1808 and it was he who rebuilt the Upper Booth farmhouse. He died in 1862 when the estates were passed on to George Cresswell, who then sold Upper Booth to William Champion.

Outlying farms around Upper Booth include Lee House Farm. This is shown on the first detailed map of the area in 1839 with a smaller house adjacent to the main range of buildings. The larger house to the east was added at a later date. The additions are shown on a map of 1880.

Further to the west is Edale Head, or Youngitt's, once the highest house in the valley. It is now a ruin. This farm probably pre-dates 1767. Alongside the packhorse route to the west was a small paddock for grazing horses and an outhouse where jaggers could rest. It was at Edale Head where Jacob Marshall lived, thought to be responsible for creating Jacob's Ladder, the short-cut stone track leading to Edale Cross and Hayfield. The last occupant left Edale Head in around 1894.

In addition to these are: Highfield Farm, the first brick structure to be built in the valley; Tags Naze (also known as Tags Neys), which was present in 1767 and featured on Burdett's map of Derbyshire of 1791; and Cartlidge Farm. The latter was present in 1880, but has since been demolished. It was situated to the north-west of Dale Head Farm and was also shown on Burdett's map of 1791, although then it was known as Dale End.

At the time of writing the National Trust owns several farms at the west end of the valley. Burdett's map clearly shows 'Over Booth' linked to 'Barber Booth' by a trackway to the north of the 'River Now'.

The Edale Booths, Their Comparative Sizes and Number of Sheep Keepers, c.1830

Booth	Acreage	Number of Sheep Owners
Whitmoorlee (Barber)	710	4
Crowdenlee (Upper)	1,582	7
Grindsbrook	1,486	9
Ollerbrook	813	3
Lady (Nether)	1,323	10
Hollins/Cold Side	600	3
Backtor	512	7

Number of Dwellings Recorded in c.1830
Source: Barnatt (1993).

Booth	Farmhouses	Smallholdings	Cottages
Upper	3	2	1
Barber	2	3	5
Grindsbrook	1	3	17
Ollerbrook	3	0	3
Nether	3	0	1

FARMS AND FARMING

Barber Booth

This is probably named after John and Richard Barber (descendants of Giles Barber who came to Edale c.1631), who are known to have owned land in the area in 1675. Formerly it has been called Whitemoreley, Whitmorelea and Whitmore-le-Booth. Whitemorelea Farm still exists in 2003, but is recorded as Barber Booth Farm in the 1842 tithe appointments.

The same document notes farms named Upper and Lower Whitemore Clough, some 500 metres to the west of Barber Booth. These are known respectively as Upper and Dore Clough, although Upper Clough has also been known as Tunnel Mouth Farm due to its proximity to the Cowburn Tunnel. The coming of the railway changed the access to Dore and Upper Cloughs, the occupants of the latter having to pass by the former. This resulted in the occupant of Dore Clough purchasing Upper Clough and letting it go to ruin in order to remove the need for traffic to pass by Dore Clough.

Littlewood Farm was shown in the same tithe schedule and, as suggested earlier, is now known as Rowland Farm, where the barn is the only traditional building left.

Manor House was formerly Eyre Barn, or Hare Barn on the 1906 Ordnance Survey map. The house was built in two parts. The back section is the older, the front being added, it is said, so that the man who lived there could attract a wife!

Ivy House was a relatively new farm as it was not noted as a farm in 1842. It is likely that buildings belonging to another holding in the booth were taken to form Ivy House Farm. At the same time Laurel Bank was noted as a small farm, as was Barley Butts.

Barber Booth.

A general view of Barber Booth.

Barber Booth, with Broadlee Bank in the background.

Above: *Group photograph taken at the rear of the shop at Barber Booth in 1930/31. Left to right, back row: Mrs R.J. Cooper, Mrs Lowe, Fred Rowbottom, Tom Nield, ?, Phyllis Rowbottom; middle row: Sarah Sims, May Nield, ?, ?, Gertie Rowbottom, Maggie Prior, Edie Carrington, Mary Allsop; front row: Ivy Rowbottom, ?.*

Left: *Morris and Brenda Oakes outside their Bakers Fold shop at Barber Booth, now closed.*

Barber Booth before the construction of the bypass.

FARMS AND FARMING

Grindsbrook Booth

Believed to have been occupied by foresters in the twelfth century, Grindsbrook Booth has undergone several changes of name. Its original name was possibly taken from a person who lived in or owned some of the property. First documented in 1342 as Grymesbroke (this original spelling appears frequently in old wills), it is thought by some to be associated with Druid rites, with, as previously noted, the prefix 'Gryms' referring to 'the evil one'.

By 1561 it was recorded as Grymes Bothy, while in 1566 a dispute in respect of a manor or farm at Grymesbrook was recorded. In the following year further reference was made to Grymsbrook in Edall, and Edall Water was also mentioned.

Grindsbrook Booth did not become the focal point of the valley until the building and establishment of a chapel there in 1633. Prior to this it was smaller than the other booths in terms of the number of farms, but had a greater number of cottages. The siting of the railway station to the south-west of the church in the nineteenth century confirmed the importance of this booth.

New Fold Farm is a relatively new holding within Grindsbrook, while the farm at Grindslow was established as the home farm for the Champion family on the Grindslow estate. Fieldhead, now the Information Centre of the Peak District National Park, was formerly Great Field Head, suggesting the presence of a large field that stretched towards Shaw Wood and Broadlee ('broad' meaning 'big', 'lea' meaning 'field') Bank. This was very probably an open field. When land was purchased at Whitmorelea in 1763 by one of the Hadfields it carried 'privileges in the open field'. This may have been for arable purposes or for grazing. Shaw Wood, to the west, is marked on Burdett's map of 1767, but it is likely that this farm is much older.

Both Small Clough and Harden Clough farms are owned by the National Trust at the time of writing. Below is an extract from the sale leaflet for Small Clough Farm when it was sold on 25 September 1946 at the Church Hotel in Edale. This gives an insight into an Edale holding at that time and an indication of land values at the middle of the twentieth century (the sale price has been handwritten at the bottom). The farm was apparently sold with a sitting tenant. Note the accuracy of the land measurement and that arable land was by order – presumably at the insistence of 'WarAg'. Lot 2 in the same sale was freehold accommodation land extending to 11 acres 0 roods 36 perches. This was 'Sold subject to an agreement in respect of the telephone kiosk for which a rental of 1/- [5p] per annum is paid.' Lot 4 was for a smallholding known as 'The Cottage' and 'Barley Butts Fields'. Totalling just over six acres, the whole lot (cottage, small range of farm buildings and the land) made £510.

Grindsbrook Booth with the Nag's Head Inn and school, c.1890.

Left: *A summer scene at Edale in 1936. Left to right: Tom Rowbottom, John Rowbottom, Harry Dakin.*

Above: *Wigley House and Fold Head in Grindsbrook Booth, c.1910.*

Right: *The village square in 1906.*

Below: *The Lodge to Grindslow House.*

FARMS AND FARMING

The Nag's Head, school and The Warren with the southern edges of the Kinder plateau behind, c.1930.

Ollerbrook Booth

The name 'Ollerbrook' is probably derived from 'the stream with the alder trees', i.e. the Oller Brook that acts as a drain from the Ashop Moor to the north. However, it is also shown as 'Otterbrook Booth' on some maps, while Burdett's map shows it as 'Older Booth'. Farming pasture at Ollerbrook is referred to in a Barber family will of 1535, with the first reference of Ollerbrook Booth being in 1562. In what was then known as 'Owlerbroke' there was a dispute over 'Stock of kine thereon, in the High Peake Lordship'.

Middle Ollerbrook Farm and Nether Ollerbrook Farm were sold by auction on 18 November 1869. At this time Mr Charles Sidebottom was the tenant, but subtenants are also noted. The sale included outbuildings, a yard, garden, orchard and three cottages, as well as the farmhouse at Middle Ollerbrook. The details for Nether Ollerbrook farmhouse stated that it was 'now converted into dwellings' and it appears that the land, extending to 306 acres 1 rood 13 perches, was attached to Middle Ollerbrook Farm. This included moorland and also '47 acres 0 roods 23 perches in an undivided Moor called 'The Nab'.' None of the enclosed ground is shown to be arable. The sale map is almost a work of art in itself.

The neighbouring landowners are shown, and these include 'The Lord Scarsdale and the Revd. John Champion' to the north-west; 'His Grace the Duke of Devonshire' to the north-east; Mr John Tym to the eastern side; John Shirt and Lorenzo Christie Esq. to the south and south-east; and Mr Joseph Taylor to the south-west. To the north of the Nab Moor is marked the Ringing Roches – an accident in the spelling, or the old name for Ringing Roger? It is not noted on these sale details who was selling the property, who purchased it, or how much the property made at sale.

The current Cote Farm, to the east of Ollerbrook, was originally built further to the north. Reasons for its re-siting are unclear. Prior to the building of Edale Mill there was a farm and corn-mill on the site. This was known as Kirk's Farm. The mill is shown on a map of 1778 and was purchased by Thomas Creswell, yeoman landowner, in 1785.

Nether Booth

In 1577 Nether Booth was known to have a hall, which is Ladybooth Hall Farm at the time of writing. Rowland Cote was to the north of Lady Booth Hall and, at the time of writing, is the site of the youth hostel. In 1791 Nether Booth is mapped as 'Neather Booth'.

In 1870 there were reports of a disagreement between Revd John Champion of Edale (landlord) and William Fiddler Mason, the outgoing tenant of Edale End. W.F. Mason was claiming that tillage and produce were the tenant's right, while the landlord argued that:

> ... stock and produce were to be retained in payment for dilapidated buildings, fences and voluntary and permissive waste done and permitted – contrary to good farming and custom of the country.

A referee, John Brittain of Fairfield, Buxton, adjudicated on 15 June 1870 that neither party had any claim.

Farming Families in Edale

The table on p35 gives an insight into the farming families in Edale in the mid-1800s. The information is incomplete as it does not indicate all the landowners of the time, and neither does it give an indication of the size of each farm. At this time the railway had not come into the valley, so self-sufficiency was still of great importance. This is characterised by the number of farms that are listed, many of which have since been amalgamated with other holdings. Out of the 43 farms listed, only 15 are still occupied by farmers at the time of writing.

Right: *Ollerbrook Lane as it leaves the booth.*

Left: *Ladybooth Farm, Nether Booth, in the 1920s.*

Grindsbrook Booth, c.1900.

Left: *Young Edale friends at Nether Booth, 1974. Left to right: Elizabeth Gilbert, Tony Gilbert, Mark Gilbert* (in pram), *Michael Goodwin, Judith Townsend, Lindsay Gilbert.*

Below: *Rowland Cote, Nether Booth, in the early 1900s, one-time home of the Batchelor family of tinned-food fame, then a youth hostel from 1947.*

FARMS AND FARMING

Farms and Their Occupants in the Nineteenth Century

Farm	Occupants, c.1842
Orchard Farm	James Atkin
Wood Farm	Thomas Burdekin
Littlewood Farm	James Carrington*
Cote Farm, Barber Booth	
Barber Booth Farm	Robert Carrington*
Shore Ground (Upper Booth) Farm	William Carrington*
Edale End Farm	John Champion*
Lady Booth Hall Farm	
Carr Farm	Joseph Cooper
Grindsbrook Farm	Elizabeth Cottrill
Upper Fulwood Farm	James Elliot
Clough Farm	Widow of Ellis Eyre
Lady Booth Farm	Rowland Eyre
Greenland Farm	
Small Clough Farm	John Froggatt
Back Tor Farm	John Gee (farmer)*
House at Upper Booth	William Hadfield*
Upper Whitmore Clough	
Lower Whitmore (Dore) Clough	James Howe
Teggs Naze Farm	John Kinder (farmer and shopkeeper)
Cote Field Farm	Matthew Marshall
Upper Holt Farm	Benjamin Nelson
Cote Farm, Upper Booth	John Pursglove
Greenhills Farm	Thomas Pursglove
Hollins Farm	Fanny Ridall
Crookstone Farm	Nathan Rowbottom
Lea House, Grindsbrook Booth	S. Rowbottom
Eyre Barn	George Shirt*
Lee House	Charles Sidebottom
Middle Ollerbrook Farm	George Sidebottom
Cote Fields Farm, Upper Booth	Isaac Sidebottom
Edale Head Farm	
Dale Head Farm	John Sidebottom
Cartlidge Farm	John Simpson (farmer and stonemason)
Harding Clough Farm	Moses Simpson (farmer and stonemason)
Waterside Farm	William Taylor*
Upper Ollerbrook Farm	
Field Head	John Tym*
Shaw Wood Farm	Micah Tym
Cote Farm, Nether Booth	
Lower Holt Farm	Thomas Tym
Nether Booth Farm	William Tym
Nether Ollerbrook Farm	Sarah Wigley

Source: Barnatt (1993)
* denotes farm owner

Left: *Grindslow House in the Grindsbrook Valley with the estate beyond, stretching up on to the moors.*

35

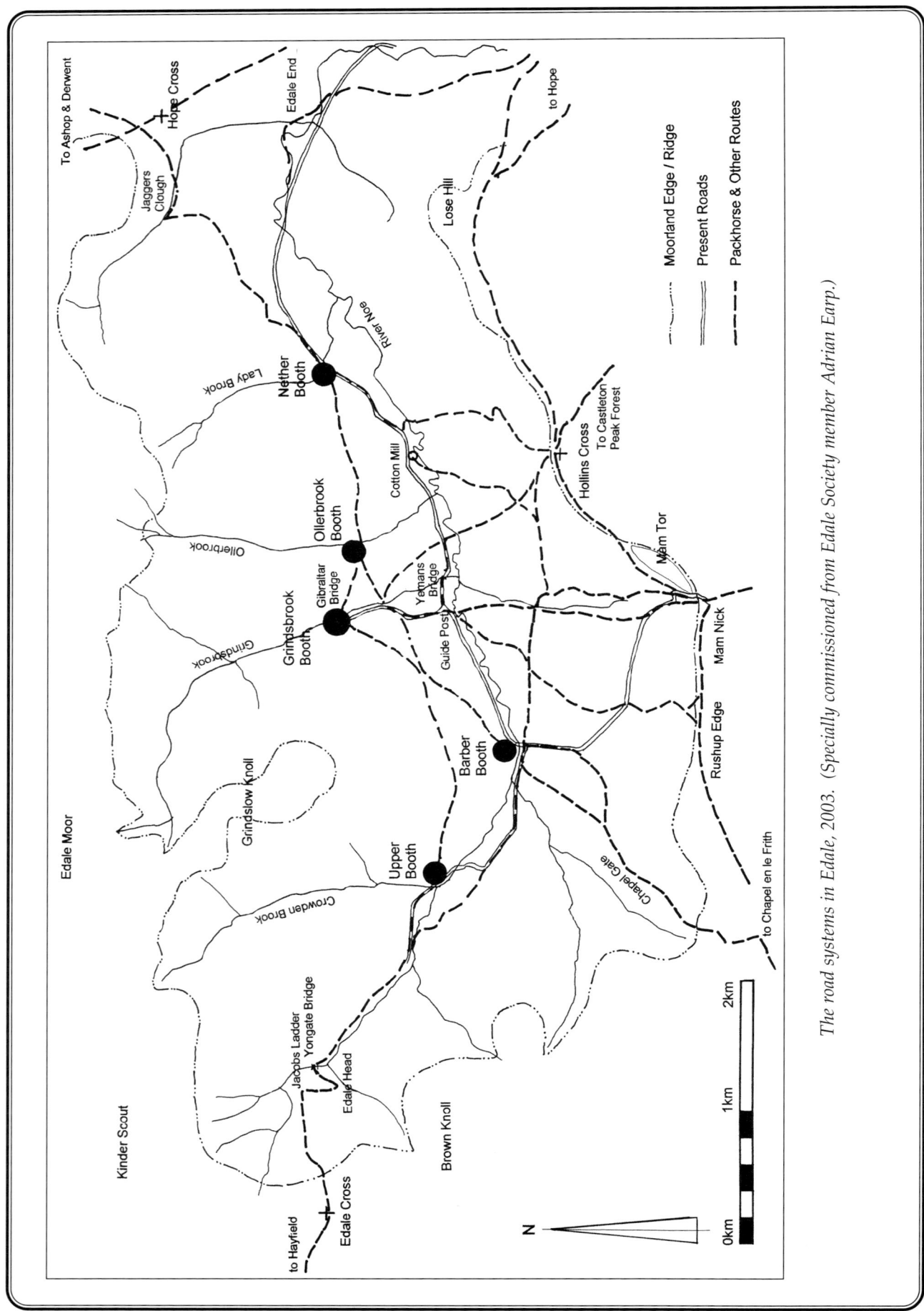

The road systems in Edale, 2003. (Specially commissioned from Edale Society member Adrian Earp.)

Chapter Three

TRANSPORT AND INDUSTRY

Edale has not escaped the impact of industrial change and social mobility. However, its unique position as a secret valley, hidden from the main Hope Valley, has meant that the impact of these changes has been gradual.

The packhorse routes, once busy and essential for trade, are now popular walking tracks for the thousands of ramblers who come to Edale. The mill, once used for grinding corn and later for spinning cotton, was converted into residential flats in 1972.

Proposals for a reservoir and a canal were abandoned, the plans for these having been relegated to the archives, along with proposals to build a steelworks. If these ideas had been implemented, Edale might have become an industrialised village with an expanding population, or a remote flooded valley. Only the railway remains, a vital link between two large cities, Sheffield and Manchester, and used by visitors and residents.

ROADS

Evidence of early-Bronze- and Iron-Age settlements are to be found on Mam Tor, on the south side of Edale – the routes used by these settlers ran along the hilltop ridges above the valley. By Norman times Edale was part of the Royal Hunting Forest but travellers still traversed the area, again sticking to high routes, often using these trackways to move between Abbey lands.

However, the first real evidence of any form of road through Edale is in the packhorse routes from the Middle Ages. Caravans of horses and mules, up to 40 or 50 strong and led by men called 'jaggers', took their salt, wool, cotton and cheese across the country from west to east and back again. Medieval travellers and pilgrims also used these tracks to move between villages and towns. As settlements started to develop in these lonely places, so did the need for trade and traffic.

THE JAGGERS' ROUTES

At this time the nearby village of Derwent, now under the water of the reservoir, was a thriving centre for trade, and the jaggers would pass through Edale, selling and exchanging their goods at this market. Their routes passed over inhospitable terrain and the jaggers walked the narrow tracks in a long line. Where there were bridges to cross, the walls of the bridges were deliberately built low to allow the animals to pass without removing the packs. There are two such bridges in Edale – Youngit (or Yongate, meaning a new bridge) Bridge and Gibraltar Bridge, both of which are of eighteenth-century construction but which would have originally have been fords or wooden bridges.

There are many stories about the men who walked these routes. The bridge at the base of Jacob's Ladder was named after Jacob Marshall, a jagger who lived at Edale Head and travelled regularly to Stockport. He would take his own route up the tiny track at Edale Head Farm, also known as 'Yongates', while the horses zigzagged up past the house. At the time of writing, halfway up the path, there are still signs of a small enclosure where the horses were kept for the night while he and his men stayed at the house. From Gilbraltar Bridge, in the centre of Grindsbrook by the Nag's Head Inn, the packhorses would travel across Jagger's Clough and on to the Hope Cross.

Until 1760 the Manchester textile trade relied on the packhorse routes for importing cotton fibre to Edale Mill, and for exporting the finished yarn. The existence of a sunken track, or 'holloway', running down towards the mill from the Mam Tor track indicates early use by this packhorse traffic. There is also a track descending to Back Tor Farm and continuing towards Hope Cross.

There is an ancient walnut tree of indeterminate age near the middle of Grindsbrook. The story goes that this was planted there so the pack animals could be tethered in its shelter to be free of the nuisance of flies, which never gather under the tree. While the animals rested the men retired to the nearby Nag's Head Inn for refreshments.

Recorded evidence shows that one of the salt routes from Cheshire ran down the Winnats Pass to Castleton and on to Hope and Hathersage. The existence of increased trade can also be seen in a petition made in 1699, by the residents of Edale, supporting the establishment of a market in Penistone. This was a centre for cattle, sheep, wool and corn which came from the eastern counties and was important because Pennine farmers grew mainly oats.

Ancient walnut tree at the entrance to Grindsbrook Booth. Thought to repel flies, these trees were often planted by the drovers so that they could tether their packhorses while resting in the nearby hostelry, in this case the appropriately named Nag's Head Inn.

Left: Gibraltar Bridge on the old packhorse route through Grindsbrook Booth with Mr Wright Dearnley's workshop up the steps on the right. The photograph was taken from the old smithy, which is the lounge of the Nag's Head Inn in 2003.

Edale Head House (also known as Yongates) and Yongates packhorse bridge from Jacob's Ladder, c.1900.

TRANSPORT AND INDUSTRY

Above: *Wooden signpost next to the old stone guidepost at the station corner, 1916.*

Right: *The detail of Hope Cross.*

Hope Cross guidepost on the packhorse route near Jagger's Clough with the Edale Valley beyond.

Even though food, clothing, fuel and building materials could be found in the valley, the outside world was beginning to have an impact. The pack-horses brought the valuable resource of salt to the valley allowing meat to be preserved for the winter months, and for use in cooking. In return the people of Edale would trade hides and wool and, in good years, oats and corn. The group of smooth stones perched above Jacob's Ladder is called the Woolpacks, so named by the jaggers because the stones reminded them of the huge packs that were carried past them.

It is thought that as the demand for cotton increased in the late-eighteenth century, a better route was required to the mill. The cutting of the Mam Tor turnpike in 1811 improved the route to Chapel-en-le-Frith. By the end of the eighteenth century trade and transport had expanded so rapidly that an Act of Parliament required guideposts to be erected on official routes, and communities were responsible for ensuring this took place.

The surviving guidepost in Edale is at the station corner and is so hidden that few are aware of its existence. It has the same patterns as the Hope Cross, which is dated 1737. The Edale guidepost shows the way to Grindsbrook Booth; to Hope via Hollins Cross; to Tideswell via Harden Clough; and to Mam Nick and Chapel via Chapel Gate. The 1839 tithe map shows the route from Grindsbrook Booth to Mam Nick via Harden Clough and the steep bridle-path.

It is believed that Chapel Gate was the original route from Edale to Chapel-en-le-Frith, and cows and sheep were driven over to the market this way. The route was made of stone, with culverts for drainage, and therefore it is presumed that carts and carriages also used this track before the road was opened.

The road in the valley naturally keeps to the northern slopes because of the maximum sunshine and also because most of the hamlets are there. The rocks of Edale are mainly sandstone and shale, and all around the valley there are signs of erosion and subsidence. This has brought problems to the only road at Edale End on the Hope Road and the traffic lights have become a semi-permanent feature as one side of the road has fallen away into the valley bottom.

The Railway

Until the coming of the railway Edale was probably one of the most remote valleys in the Pennines and the population was forced by its isolation to be fairly self-sufficient. The railway was late coming to Edale. In 1888 the Midland Railway Company gained the powers to build a railway from Dore to Chinley. There were two tunnels required on this 21-mile stretch of line. The Cowburn Tunnel at the Edale end is two miles and 82 yards long. It is believed that the original tunnel was about 400 yards longer but, because of the thinness of the roof at this point, it was thought best to open it up and create a steep culvert instead. That is why the signal-box appears to be in a strange position in relation to the tunnel and station. The line was opened to goods traffic on 6 November 1893 but did not operate the first stopping passenger service until 25 June 1894.

The schoolchildren were given a half-day holiday to celebrate the coming of the trains and according to the school records it was a wet day. It is reputed that the first person to buy a passenger ticket was an Edale resident, who was so overjoyed that he then went to the pub and drank too much!

The Midland Railway had sponsored the Dore and Chinley Company in the building of the line because they wanted a more direct route between Sheffield and Manchester, rather than the alternative route which meant travelling via Derby. In supporting the Act of Parliament needed to build the line, the Duke of Devonshire's son, Lord Edward Cavendish, described Edale as a 'very wild district' but also 'a very beautiful district with lovely views'. He was Chairman of the Highways Board of Bakewell Union and informed the House of Commons that the traction engines, bringing coal the seven miles from Chapel-en-le-Frith over the steepest roads in Derbyshire, were damaging the roads so much that many of them were impassable.

Revd Francis Beresford Champion, the local vicar, also gave evidence, saying that the cost of coal was over a guinea (£1.05) per ton in Edale, almost double the price of that in Chapel, due to the cartage cost. It would benefit the poorer inhabitants of the valley if the price could be reduced.

Cowburn Tunnel is the eighth-longest tunnel in Britain and cost £270,245 to construct, taking two-and-a-half years to build. It took 20 million bricks and 80 thousand tons of stone to complete this tunnel inside which one reaches the highest point on the line. The Totley Tunnel was built at the other end of the Hope Valley and is the second-longest tunnel in Britain. Between them the two tunnels make up a quarter of the length of the Dore and Chinley line.

A railway engine was required to assist with the building and one was brought over from Chapel along Rushup Edge, over Mam Nick and down into Edale. Crowds came to watch as the engine was steamed all the way using two lengths of track, the rear length being leap-frogged over to the front and the engine being driven forward. A team of horses towed the short length of track on a low loader. The descent of Mam Nick with a steam engine must have been a spectacular sight – crowds watched from the safety of the hilltops. It is believed that the directors of the railway company toured the line in August 1893 on the 'up' line between Edale and the Cowburn Tunnel riding on the same steam engine that was brought over the Nick.

Edale station had extensive sidings, a goods dock and coal drops. The line runs into Edale station at

TRANSPORT AND INDUSTRY

Inset: *Staff at Edale station shortly after it opened. The stationmaster often sat in the centre front, but the gentleman centre front here appears to be wearing a foreman's badge on his cap. From 1896–1905 the stationmaster was Lewis Wright.*

Above: *A steam special hauled by the Flying Scotsman passes through the Edale Valley in 1972.*

Left: *A steam locomotive at the platform of Edale station, c.1950s.*

A view towards Mam Tor and the Iron-Age fort with Manor Farm in the middle distance.

Right: *The stationmaster's house and approach to Edale station. The Church Hotel can be seen in the background.*

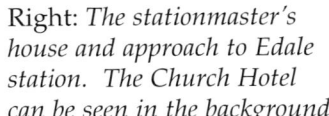

Left: *A collection of Edale train tickets including some of the first, which were issued around 1900 (top row). The rest were issued in the 1920s.*

Below: *A 'head of steam' at Edale station.*

TRANSPORT AND INDUSTRY

Railway inspection in Edale just east of the Cowburn Tunnel in 1893 prior to the opening of the line. The first steam engine, possibly this one, was brought over the Mam Tor ridge and down into the valley using a section of movable track and horses to act as a brake and move the track sections. The letters 'TO' probably stand for Thomas Oliver, one of the contractors on the line construction.

820ft above sea level with platforms on either side of a double-track main line. There were waiting-rooms on either side of the station, stone and timber built and each with a cosy fire in the winter. There was also a stationmaster's house by the bridge (the house is still there, but is privately owned at the time of writing) and full-time porters worked for the company. The booking-hall was where the modern-day café stands.

For a small village this was an excellent service with porters' rooms to lock away luggage and bicycles. Cottages were built nearby for the staff. During the war, when there was a shortage of coal and staff, villagers waited for the trains in the ticket hall where the one fire was lit. For a short time, in the summer, Midland Railway provided 'camping coaches' on the sidings, which people could rent for holiday accommodation. Families would come and stay for a week's holiday and enjoy wonderful views. The open-stone shelters are all that remain of the glorious service! The Edale signal-box remains in operation and Aaron Wheeler of Barber Booth is the signalman in 2003.

A local newspaper correspondent reported:

The opening of the local passenger, as well as goods and mineral traffic, to the villages of Edale, Hope, Bamford and Hathersage, which took place yesterday, was the cause of much rejoicing. At Edale a banner 'Success to the Chinley and Dore Railway' was conspicuous. At Hope, which is the station for Bradwell and Castleton, flags were displayed. At Hathersage the bells of the parish church were rung throughout the day. The local brass band and about 100 school children were given a ride to Edale and back. The trains to Sheffield, Manchester, Buxton and other centres of traffic were well patronised, crowds of people watched the arrival and departure of trains.

Sadly, almost 70 years after these wonderful celebrations the people of the valley were fighting to keep the line open. The passenger services were saved but the goods facilities were withdrawn on 7 October 1963 and the last regular steam-hauled freight ran in May 1968. However, freight is still carried regularly on the line. There were four steam excursions on 28 June 1994 to celebrate the opening of Edale station some 100 years earlier.

MEMORIES FROM LOCAL RESIDENTS

Local people have many stories to tell about the railway. Amy Tym and Jean Rodwell both remember when the exiled King Amanullah of Afganistan spent a night in the sidings at Edale in the 1920s. Residents say that he had a sleeping-car, a dining-car and a saloon. He appeared to be wearing striped pyjamas and his wife had on a pink dress and black hat! He waved through the window at people who had gathered to see them. Royalty once again used the line in 1967/8 when Princess Anne visited Chatsworth.

Val Gilbert recalls that during the severe winter of 1947, when the roads were completely blocked for weeks, the greengrocer (Hancocks from Bamford) and a local butcher travelled by train and set up shop on the station platform. Cattle and sheep were sent from Kirkby Stephen in wagons overnight and would arrive in Edale the next morning, and the beet pulp ration would come by train from Lincolnshire. Sheepdogs would arrive in pens from Scotland, and Val tells the story of tractors being driven in the fields and the drivers, not hearing the steam trains coming, being hit from behind by thrown lumps of coal!

Cedric Gilbert tells the story of old Fred Bunting. Fred had only one eye because he was blinded by a splinter when his father was knocking a stake into the ground. He lived in the farm at Norman's Bank in the days when there was a signal-box near the line. The steam trains would slow down at the signal and offload a ton of coal for Fred, who never paid for his fuel.

Muriel Shirt remembers when ducklings were sent from Kent to Edale by train and Cedric remembers

Snow in Edale, but the trains still run.

A 1960s steam train passes through Edale.

his mother sending calves to market by train with tags around their necks. The ten-gallon milk churns were also tagged, with the farm name and address attached. This usually took place in winter when the snow made roads impassable.

Jean Rodwell tells the story of Sam Harry Lee who was the owner of the Church Hotel, the Rambler Country House Hotel at the time of writing, before the days of Fred Heardman. Sam was an engineer in 1926 and gave up his job to drive trains during the General Strike. A school for the children of navvies was set up at Upper Booth near the Cowburn Tunnel and Mrs R.J. Cooper from Castleton came to run it. Known locally as 'Mrs R.J.', she later became headmistress at Edale School, a post she held for 36 years. She was also the church organist.

Norah McKeon remembers when secondary-school children went to New Mills Grammar School by train. During the Second World War the blinds had to be pulled down and the lights painted blue. School assembly was timed to allow for the arrival of the Hope Valley train as one third of the school pupils came from the valley. There are memories of white blouses turning to sooty grey as the trains steamed through Cowburn Tunnel.

Milly Heardman remembers that fresh fish was delivered to the Nag's Head straight from Grimsby by train. When the train arrived a local man, Harold Eyre, had to cycle up to the pub with the fish. The Nag's Head ordered a truck of coal which could be left at the sidings for two days before storage had to be paid. Clifford Cooper would then bring the coal to the inn. Vic Noblett also delivered coal in the valley.

Geoff Sims has memories of his father, Bill Sims, who worked on the railway in Edale for 47 years from the age of 14. He lived at Rose Cottage before moving to Dore Clough Farm, and from there to the shooting cabin in Grindsbrook. The shooting cabin was on the moor, a climb of a mile or so from the village, and he had to carry all the supplies he needed, including coal, by hand. Bill worked in the gang responsible for the length of track running from inside Cowburn Tunnel to the bottom of Norman's Bank.

Edward and Issac Cooper both worked on the railway, as did Jack Pryor, Jack Tym, George Wilkinson, Harold Eyre, Edward Cooper and Jack Warburton.

Margaret Wrenn first came to Edale in 1918 and her memories of working for the railway provide a fascinating insight into a service many of us would like back! Her family lived in the Mill Cottages. Margaret became a porter and office worker at the station from 1942–44, when she stood in for Harold Eyre who went into the Army. Her uniform was a divided skirt made of rough serge and a cap, which she did not wear.

Margaret's first job was to light the fires in the booking-hall and waiting-rooms before the first train went through at 6.30a.m. If the booking-hall doors were not shut the platelayers would be found warming themselves in front of the fires instead of working. Another duty was to light the platform lamps, which was difficult if it was windy. If any lights went out, the driver reported this at the next station and there would be trouble! The floors of the waiting-room were mopped and polished every day and Margaret also had to help load the milk and to board the calves going to the abattoir.

On Sunday evenings a member of the railway staff was needed to keep a close eye on the passengers on the platform because some would lower their tickets to be reused by others waiting below. To overcome this early ticket fraud, clippers were then introduced so the tickets could be punched. Wagons of barrels went off to Birmingham from Bakelite, a manufacturer of early plastics, then operating out of Edale Mill. Telegrams came into the station and were delivered by the porters. A horse dealer lived at Small Clough and his horsebox was put in the sidings at night and attached to the 10a.m. train the next morning.

Margaret's father worked at the signal-box in Edale. Her brother-in-law did a thriving trade in rabbits, and drivers and firemen would call her to place their order. She would get one shilling for each rabbit sold.

Others who lived in the railway cottages and worked for the railway included the Poulson family, the Hawtin family, Lawrence Yeardley, Jack Wright, Bill Hickinson, Jack Dakin, Issac Cooper and George Mullins. George Mullins' sister, Edith, ran a small shop in one of the cottages, and William Deacons came once a week from Hathersage to set up a bank in the end cottage. It was only possible for one customer at a time to enter and discuss their private transactions, so the rest, in all weather conditions, had to wait outside.

Fighting the Closure

In 1964 there was a proposal to close the Dore to Chinley line and the fight was on to prevent this from

TRANSPORT AND INDUSTRY

Edale station in the 1950s, when the majority of visitors to Edale came by rail.

Above: *'Pickfords Spout', named after a local family many years ago when this was the village water-supply. It became redundant in 1894 when the owners of the new railway supplied piped water to the village in return for a supply to the railway for the steam engines.*

Left: *The Church Hotel, station booking-office, stationmaster's house and Station Cottages from Small Clough track, 1918.*

Below: *The waiting-room at Edale station in the 1960s prior to demolition and replacement with concrete shelters.*

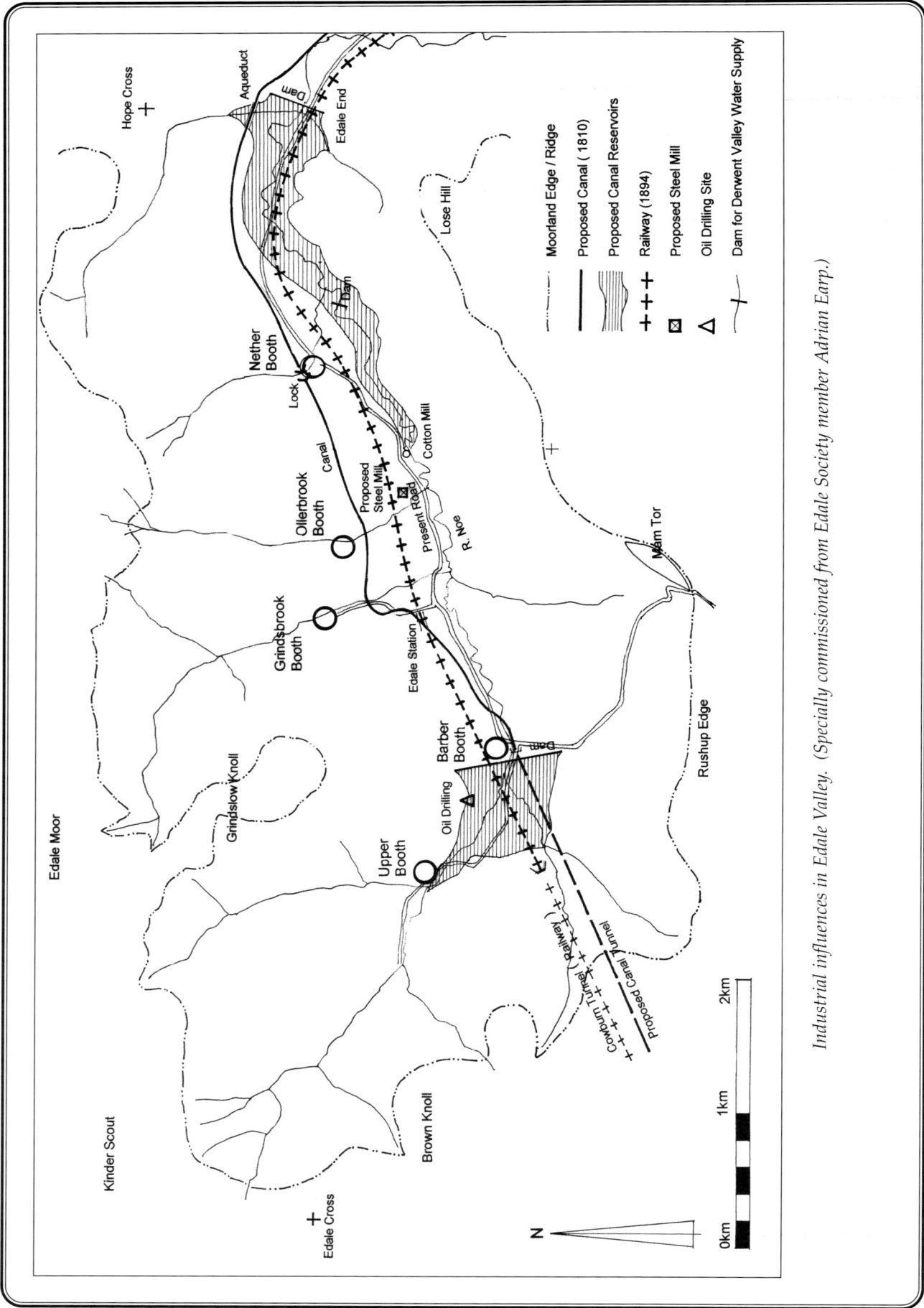

Industrial influences in Edale Valley. (Specially commissioned from Edale Society member Adrian Earp.)

TRANSPORT AND INDUSTRY

The church with Mam Tor House (formerly Endcliffe) and Belmont in the 1920s. Both houses were built after the coming of the railway in 1894. Stonecroft had not been built at the time of the photograph.

happening. Letters from that time give some insight into the hardship that this closure would have brought. A letter from the secretary of the Women's Institute, which was extremely active in opposing the closure, confirms that there were:

... 27 members, none of whom go out of the valley to work. Nine are completely dependent on public transport, with no vehicle in the family, eleven are non drivers, and private transport is only available when it is not wanted for business or farm work, three are drivers with use of a vehicle sometimes and four are owner drivers but two dislike driving in town or on wintry conditions. We have no doctor, dentist, chemist, optician, no cinema, theatre or other form of public entertainment and only 3 general shops. It will be seen that it is essential to go out of the village at times.

Barbara Castle was the Minister for Transport and the demonstration of hardship likely to be suffered if the railway was to be closed was looked on sympathetically. She had fond memories of walking in Edale and using the train service. In her response she recognised the:

... serious hardship to the residents of Edale, particularly for travel in the direction of Manchester, which would involve a circuitous road journey via Hope and, in consequence, a greatly increased journey time.

And finally she attached 'considerable importance to the preservation for recreational purposes of the means of access to the National Park by rail in the Hope Valley.'

The fight against closure was successful. The railway line continues to run at the time of writing. All the campaigning was worth it. Instead of closing the Hope Valley line, another railway line that crossed the Pennines via Glossop and the tunnel at Woodhead was closed.

THE PROPOSED CANAL

In the early-nineteenth century it was proposed to build an entire canal from a junction with the Peak Forest Canal extension (this was never made) at Chapel Milton to the junction with Cromford Canal at the south end of the Lea Wood aqueduct. The plans were deposited in the Derby archives on 30 September 1810 along with lands to be acquired and the names of owners. It would have been a mammoth feat of engineering with 12 locks climbing between Chapel Milton and Cowburn Tunnel (149ft). The eastern end of the tunnel was opposite but just west of Barber Booth, and it went down the valley to 'Mr Champion's in Edale at Lady Booth'. The canal was planned to follow the valley with a series of locks, always on the left bank, until it reached Baslow. Here it was to cross to the right and continue to Bubnell, then on through Bakewell, Matlock and Cromford.

Former Edale resident Richard Nicholson researched the plans for this canal and made a comparison between the canal and railway route which was to come some 84 years later. He noted that at Barber Booth the proposed canal exit was below the level of the future railway but that the canal and railway would have been destined to meet at the site of the future Edale station. The proposed waterway then cut diagonally across the lawn in front of the Church Hotel, crossed the village road by an aqueduct and began to diverge from its contour. It entered a shallow but deepening cut before turning gently left past the site of what is Cooper's Bungalow at the time of writing, then under the road and into the field in front of Church Inn (Church Cottage at the time of writing).

It crossed the road yet again and passed behind Field Head, travelling on an aqueduct over Grindsbrook, and to the first lock behind Shirt's farmhouse at Nether Booth.

Three reservoirs were to be built: Perry Foot, outside the valley near Sparrowpit, which was the smallest and was to supply the summit; Barber Booth, which was to be quite large and was to extend

A steam locomotive passes Edale signal-box during the village celebration of the railway centenary in 1994.

Families outside the Mill Cottages in 1906.

Edale 'Band of Hope' in 1916.

TRANSPORT AND INDUSTRY

to Upper Booth; and Edale End, the largest, which was to extend from a dam east of Edale End and along the valley beyond Nether Booth. Carr House would have been flooded and the road below Clough Barn would have gone too, but with no proposal of where the road would have been re-routed.

The plans remain in the Derby archives, despite all the initial work and detailed recording of land ownership. The railways superseded the canals and it is interesting to reflect on how different Edale could have been with a canal rather than a railway running through the valley.

EDALE MILL

The tax records of 1778 record that there was already a working mill in Edale, probably from the turn of the eighteenth century when Edale House was built. It appears that a Thomas Cresswell of Crowden-le-Booth, a yeoman farmer and landowner, bought the land and buildings surrounding the existing mill in 1785. It had been known as Kirk Farm and covered an area of 70 acres, which included a blacksmith's shop. It seems that this farm was owned by a Robert Kirk (blacksmith), Robert Iberson and Abraham Iberson. As oats were the main crop grown in the valley, it seems probable that this original mill was used to grind corn brought on packhorses by the jaggers.

The mill had a good supply of water from the River Noe and when corn ceased to be carried into the valley it became a tannery with hides supplied from the skinning 'factory' at Skinner's Hall. Skinner's Hall, built in the early-eighteenth century, is a residence at the time of writing. Remains of the old hooks and pulleys can be found in the upper rooms.

Nicolas Cresswell, Thomas' son, lived in America from 1774 until 1777 where he met a man named Kirk, who was the son of the blacksmith of Edale. On his return, and not wanting to farm, Cresswell eventually took over the lease of the mill in 1793 for 99 years. To do this he took out a mortgage, borrowing the money from a Peter Nightingale of Lea 'in fee of House, Land and Cotton Mill £1,500'.

Aerial view of Edale Mill and Edale House.

Edale Mill, 1919.

The old mill was incorporated into a newer structure, a rectangular gritstone building, four stories high with a low-pitch roof. This new mill was used to produce cotton as the industry spread through the Pennine valleys. A large millpond was constructed and sluice-gates built to control the river flow behind Skinner's Hall. There were more sluice-gates beside the Mill Cottages, and the water runs under these cottages towards the pond.

Arkwright looms were installed and all the raw materials were brought to the mill via the packhorses travelling between the large cities. The bells of the leading horse were a familiar sound in the valley, and the finished lace thread was carried back over the routes to the urban centres. Nicholas Cresswell owned the mill for only a short time and died in about 1804.

There is evidence of the release of a mortgage on the mill in 1802 to a Robert Blackwell, mercer and draper of Wirksworth.

Kirk's Farm including the cotton mill, with an agreement for absolute purchase by Robert Blackwell for the sum of £2,600 out of which £1,500 due and owing to Peter Nightingale is to be paid off.

Work in the mill was done mainly by women and children. Although a few may have lived in the valley, the majority walked over Hollins Cross from Castleton on a daily basis and in all weathers. This journey involved a loss of working time, especially in winter, and resulted in the mill owner building houses near the mill, the first six of the Mill Cottages being built near the highway. Robert Blackwell died shortly afterwards and his widow sold the mill in 1835 to Hector Christie.

The story of one particular family arriving in Edale to work in the mill can be traced through the 1841 Census. William Elliot, his wife Ann and their eight children came to Edale from Kent to work in the mill in the 1830s. At first they lived in Grindsbrook and Ann and six of the children worked in the mill as cotton or lace-thread workers. The youngest, Mary, aged nine, worked as a cotton cleaner – a particularly dangerous job that led to the early death of many young girls. By 1851 the family

Vitus Villa (now Glen Tor) and Ruskin Villa, homes to the Jackson family.

Above: *Mr Smith, the shopkeeper at the Mill Cottages, Marjorie and Dorothy Smith and Kath Belfitt, c.1910.*

Below: *Edale Mill manager Eber Jackson, c.1905.*

TRANSPORT AND INDUSTRY

Edale mill dam.

had moved to one of the Mill Cottages, the father was the mill postman, and the rest of the family was also employed in the mill. May Davis, who is 100 years old at the time of writing, came to live in Edale at the age of seven and recalls passing the Irish navvies working on the roads as she went to work in the mill for 2p an hour. She would also walk the 12-mile return trip to Chapel-en-le-Frith with her mother to do the shopping, returning with heavy bags that often broke. Another centenarian, Martha Tym, who lived in the Mill Cottages, often spoke of the hardships of working as a young girl in the mill for long hours and small recompense.

In 1885 the 'cotton mill, tenements (6), land and habitation' were sold to Hector Christie, a Scotsman, for £2,200. Hector and his son Eber lived in the big house adjacent to the mill, known as Edale House. A William Jackson, living at Skinner's Hall, was appointed as manager. The job stayed in the family for three generations and was passed on from William to Eber to Hector Jackson. Hector remained at the mill until it finally closed in 1934.

Hector Christie sold Edale Mill in 1898 to the Fine Spinners and Doublers Company Ltd, but retained some of the surrounding land. A few men were needed at the mill at this time for maintenance work, and their families lived in the row of cottages, which was extended by another 15 cottages around the turn of the century. Two new bridges were built over the River Noe at Back Tor and Lower Hollins farms. Hector Christie sold some of his land to the east of the mill, and two houses – Ruskin and Vitus Villas (now Glen Tor) – were built. The purchasers were William and Eber Jackson.

The mill was converted to steam after the construction of the Manchester to Sheffield railway line in 1894. Lighting was supplied by candles, and work often continued throughout the night. Before its closure the mill had begun to specialise in fine 'doubled' thread for lace manufacture in the towns of Derby and Nottingham. However, foreign competition, rising costs and the relative isolation of the mill led to its demise.

Tony Jackson remembers that his father continued to be employed by the company from 1934–38, even though the mill was closed. The intention was for Hector to dismantle all the equipment in the mill, to pack it up and send it by train to a mill in Settle, where the company was then based. It was intended that he should follow and manage this mill, but by this time Hector had decided to join the RAF as a store man and he continued to live at Peace Haven (now Grayling) in Edale until 1956.

After its closure the mill was for a short time a storehouse for Bakelite. During the war it provided temporary housing for surviving soldiers returning from Dunkirk and accommodated up to a 1,000 men. There were no baths in the mill and Tony Jackson remembers his parents offering their bathroom to the soldiers, as did other families with facilities. The mill finally fell into disrepair in the 1950s.

The Landmark Trust bought Edale Mill in 1973. It was converted into flats and has been lived in ever since. The large millpond is overgrown with alder and silver birch and has become a haven for wildlife.

STORIES OF THE RESIDENTS

Clive Wetherall recalls that the mill owner, Hector Christie, did not want to see the back of the workers' cottages with their kitchens and outside toilets facing his house. Consequently, one of the rows was built back-to-front, so the front of the row faced his house.

Sue Favell remembers the story about a Mrs Smith (Margaret Wrenn's mother) who lived in one of the Mill Cottages. She had four daughters and one son. Every day she would cook sausages and mash for the factory girls who walked over from Castleton to work in the mill; in winter their lanterns shone down from the hillside.

Tony Favell recounts the fact that in the nineteenth century orphans used to work in mills and that some may have been employed in Edale. It is believed that some were sent down from Edinburgh and other parts of the country and lived for a time at Skinner's Hall.

Chris Jackson has vivid memories of growing up in Edale. He remembers the mill as being the largest building in the valley, albeit derelict and out of use. It held lots of mysteries and was a fun place to wander around, especially the overgrown water dam in which bulrushes had established themselves.

The ridge marking the south side of the valley and the parish, with Lose Hill, Back Tor and the Mill Cottages.

Left: Ladies in their 'Sunday best' at the mill, c.1900.

Right: Sports day at Edale Mill, c.1910, with mill manager Eber Jackson in the background.

Left: Mill girls and lads take a break, c.1910.

Right: Mill ladies, c.1900. Including, left to right, back row: Nellie Hulse, Mrs Maudsley and Louise Jackson (the wife of the mill manager).

TRANSPORT AND INDUSTRY

Edale Mill after its conversion to flats by the Landmark Trust in 1973.

James William Carrington in front of the experimental oil drill at Barber Booth, 1935/36.

Tony Jackson tells the story of his aunt, Hannah Harvey, Eber's sister, who moved out of Vitus Villa and into a bungalow called Lee Croft, which used to be down the mill lane and behind the two houses. It was originally built for the foreman of the mill, Fred Burrows, and Mrs Harvey preferred it to Vitus Villa. She took in paying guests and was a teacher in Hayfield, Edale and Castleton. In 1939 she rented out Vitus Villa to Bill Noblett, who kept pigs in the backyard. Trouble broke out between them because the pigs made an unwelcome mess when she had guests in the bungalow. Bill moved out to Small Clough Farm and Vitus Villa was sold to the Derwent Valley Water Board. The bungalow was pulled down by the Water Board in 1947.

THE PROPOSED STEELWORKS

A proposal in 1938 by the steel firm Messrs Brown Bayleys Ltd to build a steelworks on 'a narrow strip of land between the Hope Road, Edale, and the railway' caused great controversy in the valley. The company intended to produce light steel for aeroplane wings.

Edale parish councillor Isaac Cooper, along with the majority of his colleagues, wanted the steelworks in the valley. In fact, most of the residents agreed with him, feeling that a new industry would bring employment into the valley. There was a petition in Edale of 177 signatures, and fewer than 20 residents objected to the proposed works.

In 1939 Isaac Cooper chaired a parliament in the village square. He sat at a baize table facing the villagers, some of whom were sitting on rows of wooden benches, others leaning against the stone wall. A newspaper reporter described the scene:

Farm girls left their milking, farmers their flocks. They walked to an open stretch of ground flanked by the village post office, the village inn and the school to hear the parish councillor's views.

At a meeting of the Rural District Council in Chapel-en-le-Frith, Isaac Cooper continued his campaign. In an impassioned speech he asked: 'I wonder how many members of the council have experienced the anxiety and worry which parents of Edale have suffered when their children are working away?'

However, those in favour of the steelworks were up against a formidable alliance. Those opposed to the scheme included The Ramblers Federation (Manchester and District Branch); 200 Members of Parliament; Sheffield City Council; the Council for the Preservation of Rural England; and Fred Heardman of the Church Hotel, Edale, who was also chairman of the Edale Parish Council. Fred argued that many of the men employed in the proposed steelworks would be bussed in from outside the valley, and that local people would not benefit at all.

The main argument from The Ramblers Federation was that:

... the indiscriminate industrialisation of rural areas and uncontrolled development is in the long run detrimental to the interests of the country. Many members come from areas where vast works are lying idle or derelict and we want to see the industrial parts of the country once more reach prosperity in which rural communities would share... it is a mistaken idea to take advantage of lower rates and wages while cities and towns have derelict works and mills, depressed populations, unable like rural residents even to raise garden produce for themselves.

Sheffield City Council shared this view based on its own experiences in the slums in the city. They wanted the works sited in area of depressed employment where social services already existed.

A PROPOSAL TO FLOOD THE VALLEY

At the beginning of the twentieth century plans were afoot to flood Edale as part of the development of six

Above: *The site of the proposed steelworks near Edale Mill Cottages.*

Right: *An extract from the* Chronicle *– 'The Lights go on in Edale.'*

Below: *The inauguration of Edale Dam at Nether Booth in April 1951. Following a decision that the Edale Valley was unsuitable for a reservoir, the dam was built to collect and take water through a pipeline to Ladybower reservoir in the adjoining Snake Valley. Many of the workers came from Ireland, and Pat Wrenn (standing immediately to the right of the flag pole) remained in Edale when he married Margaret Smith from the shop at the Mill Cottages.*

CHRONICLE

THURSDAY, NOVEMBER 16, 1950 — ONE PENNY

Edale Parish Church is floodlit

Nags Head Inn has electric lanterns

THE LIGHTS GO *ON* IN EDALE

EDALE (Derbyshire), Wednesday.

Lights shone bravely through uncurtained windows here tonight: from cottages and farms beacons shone into the darkness. Modernity—and electricity—had at last caught up with this rural parish of 390 people.

Tonight Edale celebrated the Great Switch-on.

Silver-haired Mrs. Grace Elliott, 89, who claims to be the oldest inhabitant, climbed the steep hill from her cottage to see the sights.

Coloured fairylights twinkled outside Parker's Cafe in the village square, where the local lads and lasses danced until 1 a.m.

The floodlit parish church blazed like a beacon across the lovely Hope Valley.

In the Nag's Head—which first had its licence 373 years ago—the landlord, Mr. Frederick Herdman—served by the light of electric lanterns.

"We tried to get electricity in 1938," he said, "and in 1939 work should have started, but the war stopped it.

"We appealed after the war and work started in the village just a month ago.

"Before that we used to have oil lamps in here, and in the living quarters we had electricity generated by our own plant."

At the dance the chairman of the parish council, Mr. Edward W. Elcock, thanked the Electricity Board for bringing its wares to the parish.

The profits of the dance are to go to the Creswell Colliery Disaster Fund.

Footnote: Edale had its first-ever power cut yesterday morning. It lasted one hour.

Mrs. Grace Elliott
Oldest inhabitant

Borrowdale, the lovely Valley of the Birches, cannot have electricity yet. The Electricity Board has written that the cost is prohibitive, as capital expenditure will allow only for supplying industry, agriculture, maintenance and housing estates.

The estimated cost of underground cable is £59,800, compared with £1,643 three years ago, and the present estimate for all overhead cable is £24,700, and for pare overhead and part underground £33,900.

TRANSPORT AND INDUSTRY

dams on the Derwent. In the event, only three dams were built and Edale escaped because the bedrock was found to be too unstable and the valley too wide.

The original plans show that the dam wall was to be built at Edale End and the whole valley was to be flooded right up to Upper Booth. Fortunately, the survey showed that the bedrock was not suitable, and the plan was abandoned.

However, in 1947 the Derwent Valley Water Board began to purchase properties to the south of the road from Nether Booth to Skinner's Hall. This coincided with the Duke of Devonshire's estate having to sell its land in Edale to meet crushing death duties. Some properties were compulsorily purchased, Hector Jackson's house, Peace Haven, being one of them. Once again, rumours abounded. Had the dam proposal been resurrected?

In the event, the dam did not happen. What actually happened was the opening of a pipeline from Edale to Ladybower reservoir. The pipe is tall enough to walk along and Alan Atkins walked the whole length of the pipeline before water started to flow. A small reservoir was built behind Nether Booth and Lady Booth Farms, with a sluice-gate to control the flow of water. Vents along the length of the pipe allow the Water Board to monitor water quality, the Water Board being responsible for the sewage levels in the river.

The reason for the purchasing of houses along the stretch of the river had been to give the Derwent Valley Water Board access rights. Eventually all the houses were sold back into private hands, Ruskin Villa and Glen Tor being the last houses to be sold by Severn Trent Water in the 1990s.

ELECTRICITY COMES TO EDALE

Edale was one of the last valleys in Derbyshire to get electricity. A supply had been expected in 1939, but the war postponed its introduction. In the meantime only the Church Hotel, possessing its own generator, had electricity. The rest of the community relied on oil-lamps, candles, wood and other solid fuel.

Before the Yorkshire Electric Power Company could extend their mains from Hope they needed a guaranteed number of applicants, and this entailed canvassing every household in the valley. A debate raged about how the supply would be provided. Initially, in the 1930s, it had been decided that there would be overhead cables, but there was concern about preserving the beauty of the valley. It was a familiar issue. Edale was eventually switched on in 1950.

PEAT CUTTING

As the valley was gradually cleared of trees to make way for settlements, wood became increasingly scarce and peat was used instead for cooking and heating. The cutting and stacking of the peat for the winter took place at the same time as haymaking, when the weather was relatively dry. At Grindsbrook Booth, the Peat Lane still marks the route of the sledges, which brought the peat down from Peat Moor. Two peat pools, areas from which the peat was cut, can still be seen on the tops and are relics of this peat-cutting era.

Farms with a north-facing slope had no direct route to the Peat Moor, but at the end of the nineteenth century they had right of access to the moors and the peat. Hope Parish had a narrow 'panhandle' of access, running up on to the north-east corner of Kinder, giving them access to the moors.

QUARRYING

Although the stone walls in Edale are built from locally quarried stone, there has never been an important commercial quarry in the valley. Some of the railway bridges were built out of stone from Jagger's Clough, and it is thought that Edale Church was built from stone quarried at Nether Tor and brought down on sledges.

However, the stone used in most of the larger houses and buildings in Edale was imported, although one or two barns built without mortar are made from local stone. Also, a local shale-like sandstone found in sheets of an inch thick has been used as a roofing material.

Stone was quarried out of the ground for local use, leaving channels and small shallow hollows. Looking down towards Grindsbrook from Peat Moor these can still be seen at the time of writing.

THE SMITHY, THE SAWMILL AND THE SAW-PIT

There have been at least four blacksmiths operating out of Edale. One was on the site of Kirk's Farm at Edale Mill, where records show that Hector Christie converted the blacksmith's shop on purchase of the mill. Another was at Church Cottage, in a building adjoining the house, and the third was in what is, at the time of writing, the lounge bar of the Nag's Head Inn. A fourth smithy was situated at Upper Booth. From their importance in the days of the packhorse

The completed dam with Nether Booth in the background.

drovers these smithies gradually disappeared with the coming of motorised traffic.

Two sawmills are remembered in the village, and there would probably have been others. Clive and Elizabeth Wetherall recall that a sawmill once operated from their house, Glen Thorn, which was then owned by the Angus brothers. This was a working mill from 1953 until 1963. There was also a saw-pit in front of the Nag's Head in the 1930s. At that time a saw-pit and workshop were situated in what is now Hillock Cottage, run by Wright Dearnley, a joiner who lived in nearby Warren Cottage. Before that, the business was owned and run by the Rowbottom family. Everything from doors to windows to farm carts was made and repaired in this workshop. Wright Dearnley was also the local undertaker, and would make coffins to order.

The 1891 Census

An analysis of the 1891 Census reveals a great deal about the impact of industry on the Edale Valley. The Census shows a population of 955 (627 males and 318 females) of which 631 were identified as being associated with the railway. While the majority of the workers and their families were housed in railway huts or the navvy hut at Nether Meadow, some were boarders or lodgers with local families, thus providing welcome income.

The civil engineer for this enormous project was a Mr Herbert Hall of Sheffield, and he had only one inspector, two overseers and three foremen with which to co-ordinate and direct an army of tunnel miners, platelayers, stonemasons, blacksmiths, brickmakers, bricklayers, carpenters, carters, labourers and navvies. Other interesting occupations included 'Missionary to the Navvies' and 'Rope runner'.

Intriguingly, very few of the 324 villagers (of whom 195 were native to Edale) were employed on the railway. Issac Cooper, farmer and innkeeper, was the oldest villager at 86, and the oldest woman was Widow Hannah Marrison, who was 81. Tyms, Shirts, Lowes, Coopers and Burdikins were prominent local families – names still in evidence at the time of writing. Although less numerous, the Hadfields, Carringtons and Rowbottoms had also long been established in Edale.

It is not surprising to find that the main occupation amongst the local male population at this time was farming, with 45 per cent being farmers or farm labourers, while 50 per cent of employed females were in domestic service. The cotton-mill was a large employer with three male and ten female employees from the valley, with the rest coming from Castleton and further afield. The mill manager was William Jackson and the mechanic was Bob Marshall. Miss Edna Tym was employed to 'dauble', whilst Master Arthur Tym 'doffed'.

Edale residents also included nine skilled tradesmen, three grocers, two schoolmasters, two police constables, two gamekeepers and a post boy. Francis Champion, Clerk in Holy Orders, lived with his wife, mother, two daughters, four sisters, housemaid, cook, laundress and coachman in some comfort at Grindslow House. The vicarage (the Old Parsonage) was unoccupied.

There were 58 children of school age (4–13) but this rose to 138 if the railway children were included. Of these children, 99 were classed as scholars, which infers that the rest were either truants or were employed!

The population in Edale in 2003 is around 350.

The Edale Valley from the sled road, once used to transport peat from Peat Moor to Grindsbrook Booth and later for the construction of a water-supply on Grindslow Knoll.

Packhorse route at Gibraltar Bridge in Grindsbrook Booth. A saw-pit and woodyard is on the right adjoining an old smithy.

Chapter Four

Two World Wars

Edale lost 12 young men in the First World War, a significant number for such a small community. They were:

Capt. A.D Montague Brown
Major T.C. Jowett
Corp. G.A. Lowe
Lce Corp. S.E.B. Lowe
Gdsman F. Marrison
Pte W. Robins
Pte C. Robinson
Pte R.E. Robinson
Pte T.H. Rowbottom
Pte W.P. Shirt
Gdsman L.J. Smith
Capt. S. Watts.

The war brought many changes to village life. Many of the men were away fighting. There were massive Army camps in the valley, and the fields were scattered with tents and temporary barracks. One of the largest camps was at Barber Booth at the foot of Mam Tor below Rowlands Farm. The rifle range remains on the hillside above Chapel Gate.

The years following the war brought yet more changes. For generations Edale had been a farming community, but all this looked likely to change in 1935/6 when a trace of oil was found in the area between Barber Booth and Upper Booth. Drilling took place in a field to the east of 'The Tips' at the mouth of the Cowburn Tunnel. This exploration continued for about two years, but despite much excitement drilling was declared to be uneconomic.

As this exploration closed down, Edale became excited once more when, the following year, Brown Bailey Steel Co. proposed to build a steelworks in a field opposite the Mill Cottages, close to the railway. There was a lot of opposition from many quarters, although most of the locals could see advantages, particularly the prospect of employment. However, in the end, planning permission was refused and the steelworks were built elsewhere.

It was about this time, in 1936, that a summer camp for the unemployed was opened in a field between the Mill Cottages and Skinner's Hall. Groups of the unemployed spent two weeks at the camp and this continued every year until 1939.

During the 1930s, and before the National Health Service, medical care was either provided by private means, a collective, or through a friendly society or similar organisation. Edale was served during these years by the Ancient Order of Foresters, through which members would be allocated to a doctors' 'panel' for attention and treatment. A similar arrangement applied to hospitalisation and families were covered by the 'Penny in the Pound' contributions run through friendly societies. In addition, 'Hospital Sundays' were a regular feature, when money was collected to raise financial support for local hospitals.

Arthur Dakin during the First World War.

THE BOOK OF EDALE

Edale Army camp at Barber Booth in 1906.

Army camp at Barber Booth in the late 1920s.

Left: *The Territorial Army camp behind the Church Hotel in the early 1900s.*

Below: *Sunday parade at the Barber Booth military camp, c.1900.*

TWO WORLD WARS

THE SECOND WORLD WAR

The beginning of hostilities in 1939 brought the 'blackout' to all parts of the country and this was strictly observed in the Edale Valley. Evacuees arrived from Manchester and were allocated homes in the village where room was available. Some remained throughout the war years, but many returned home when the fear of heavy bombing declined. Food rationing was introduced at this time and later clothes rationing was also imposed.

The Second World War changed most things in the country, and Edale was no exception. Various firms in the area were recruiting staff to work in war-related industries in the Hope Valley, Sheffield and Chapel-en-le-Frith. Among these were: Metro-Vickers, Bamford; Newburgh Engineering, Bradwell; Ferodo, Chapel-en-le-Frith; Cooke and Stevensons, Brough; G & T Earles, Hope.

Conscription of men to the Armed Forces started to have its effect as men between the ages of 18–26 who were not in reserved occupations were called up. Flight Sergeant Alan Tym of Edale lost his life during the war. Women quickly took over work previously done by men and as conscription was extended to cover ages 26–40 this change continued.

The Dunkirk evacuation had its effect on the village as the closed cotton-mill was taken over in June 1940 to accommodate some of the evacuated troops. Many appeared to be from artillery regiments as two Howitzer field guns were set up in the mill grounds near the main road for training purposes. Some time later the mill was taken over by Bakelite to store products. Bill Povey was the local manager for this firm.

Before the war started in 1939 an RAF plane crashed on Broadlee Bank. This was to be the first of many – a number of planes crashed on the moors around Edale. A barrage balloon escaped from its moorings near Sheffield and came to ground in the Edale Valley. Salvage materials from the balloon were used by locals to make clothing and as tarpaulins.

The Home Guard was formed in 1940 and Edale had its share of colourful local members. Wilf Hulse, with his walrus moustache, is remembered by many, and his Home Guard activities were talked about for years. Wilf was renowned in the valley as 'Mister Fixit' and drove a Jowett car which often tipped over on bends. He would simply climb out and tip it back onto its wheels. Heating in the car was provided by an upright oil heater situated in the well of passenger seat. One story about Wilf relates to the Mill Cottages, where he lived. The cottages had a line of privies along the back of the houses facing the road. Wilf was tired of the smell emanating from his privy and poured some petrol down it before throwing in a match. He was unaware that the line was connected until an old lady rushed out of the adjoining privy with her clothing on fire!

The Women's Voluntary Service was formed in Edale about this time, bringing together the Women's Institute and the Mothers' Union, who had previously worked separately but, when combined, proved formidable. They saw to the fair distribution of food which was not available in the shops, as well as undertaking other voluntary work associated with housing and assistance to the elderly.

Car ownership in Edale had increased before the war but petrol rationing made things very difficult. Petrol coupons were allocated according to work requirements and other essential needs. The train service during the war years ran with the same frequency as it does at the time of writing. Trains were hauled by steam locomotives which, coming from the direction of Hope, could be identified by plumes of smoke as the labouring engines pulled their way up Norman's Bank into the Edale Valley. Many will remember Alf Harrison and Margaret Smith (later Wrenn) who worked at the station during the war years.

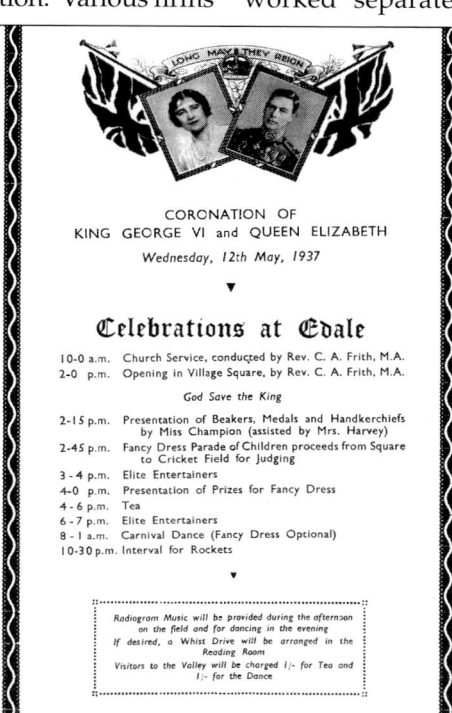

Programme for Edale's coronation celebrations in 1937.

WARTIME ENTERTAINMENT

Before the war there were few activities for the young people of the village. Boy Scouts and Girl Guides were introduced in the early 1930s but did not last long. The hut they used was situated between Cooper's Barn and Lime Field, opposite the school. Both the church and chapel held Sunday schools aimed at children of school age. The Reading Room situated behind the Nag's Head public house was mainly for men and youths, with a snooker table, dartboard and mini library. This room was also used for mixed social occasions and meetings.

A dancing club was formed in 1942 by Mrs Corrigan in the Church Hotel Café (The Rambler at the time of writing) and this proved popular. The aim was to teach young people how to dance so they could enjoy social events. Dances were held at various local venues, including: the Memorial Hall,

Above: *Edale May Queen, 1935.* Left to right: Ros Rowbottom, Amy Tym, Hazel Jackson, Joan Sweet, Brenda Wilson (Queen), ?, Thomas Maudsley, Margaret Rowbottom, Pat Gilbert (small girl in front), Rosamund Burdikin, Lilian Cooper, Doreen Gilbert.

Left: *Crowning of Edale May Queen, 1933/4.* On stage: Joan Sweet, George Goodwin, Ruth Tym (Queen), ?, Noel Davies, Phoebe Scholey, Hazel Jackson.

TWO WORLD WARS

Bradwell; Loxley Hall, Hope; Mechanics' Institute, Bamford; Peak Pavilion, Castleton; and occasionally at Edale School. The dances in Edale were organised by Mrs Greenstreet, whose son Neville, together with Peggie Day of Ollerbrook, provided the music. Peggie's husband, Albert, ran the taxi service and school-bus service during the war.

Some teenagers joined the Air Training Corps at Hope, where parades and training took place on two evenings and every Sunday of each week. Apart from drill parades, cadets were taught Morse code, aircraft recognition, basic navigation, and other subjects associated with the RAF. There were also occasional visits to RAF stations. These sometimes included short flights, which evoked interest and enthusiasm.

During 1943 airborne troops came to train in Edale, and this continued until September 1944. Edale became a very attractive place to visit, especially for the girls of the Hope Valley. Many social events were held in the village at this time and Army transport was used to take locals to and from these events.

Various National Savings promotions were held during the war years. These promotions, held to help finance the war effort, were called 'Aircraft' or 'Warship' weeks, and each village, district or town had its target, whether it was for a torpedo boat or a Spitfire. (A Spitfire cost £25,000 at the time.)

As the war came to an end in 1945, so the village returned to normal, but rationing and shortages continued for some years.

WHERE WE LIVED

The chart on the following pages shows who was living where in Edale during the later years of the Second World War.

Left: *Edale May Queen, 1932.*

Below: *Edale School May Queen, 1932/3. Left to right, back row: ?, Beryl Howe, Rosmund Rowbottom, Hazel Jackson, Margaret Rowbottom, Rosamund Burdikin, Lilian Cooper; front row: Jeannie Hawtin, Norah Rowbottom, Margaret Dakin, ?.*

Above: *Edale School May Queen, 1933.*

Opposite, bottom: *The Home Guard during the Second World War.* Pictured are: *David Naylor* (first left, back row), *Jim Carr* (fifth from left, back row), *Jack Prior* (first left, front row) *and Wilf Hulse* (third from left, front row).

Edale School May Queen, 1935.

61

Edale Houses and Farms – Occupants 1938–42

Booth	Lee House and Farm	Arthur Mallinson
Upper Booth	The Orchard Farm	Robinson
" "	Upper Booth Farm	Greta Shirt
" "	Crowden Lea Cottage	
" "	Crowden Cottage	
" "	Arnfield Cottage	Charles Cooper
" "	Highfield Farm	Robert Smith
" "	Dale Head Farm	William Sims
" "	Dore Clough Farm	Sam Tym
" "	Manor House Farm	Harry Scholey (postman)
Barber Booth	Littlewood Cottage	William Carrington
" "	Whitmore Lea Farm	Proctor
" "	Whitmore House	James Carrington
" "	Ivy House Farm	Jack Tym
" "	Barley Butts Cottage	Herbert Morrow
" "	Barber Booth Shop (Bakers Fold)	Sam Marrison
" "	Barnsfold Cottage	Coghills
" "	Laurel Bank (Holly Cottage)	Sam Tym (Nields)
" "	Brookfield	Davis/Oakes
" "	Rowland Farm	Scott/Hunter
" "	Barber Booth Café (Riverside)	Jack Prior
" "	Broadlee Bungalow	Joseph/Edward Cooper
" "	Waterside Farm	Percy Broome
Station	Small Clough Farm	Ritchie Bramwell
" "	Upper Holt Farm	William Critchlow
" "	Shaw Wood Farm	Nicholas Tym/Wilsons
" "	Glenthorn House	Ernest Chapman
" "	Harden Clough Farm	Rileys
" "	Greenlands Farm	Richard Cooper
" "	1 Station Cottages	Isaac Cooper
" "	2 Station Cottages	Jack Dakin
" "	3 Station Cottages	Mullins
" "	4 Station Cottages	Paulson
" "	5 Station Cottages	Bingham
" "	6 Station Cottages	Walker/Dobbs/Frankish
" "	Station House	Heardman
" "	Church Hotel	Hickley
Station to Grindsbrook	Bungalow (Plevna)	Revd Frith
" "	Vicarage	James Cooper
" "	Bungalow (Barnfield)	Middleton
" "	Field Head Bungalow	Pembertons
" "	Field Head	Burdikin
" "	Church Cottage	Elcock
" "	The Meads	Walker/Wragg
" "	The Hermitage	Hornsby
" "	Endcliffe (Mam Tor) House	R.J. Cooper
" "	Belmont	Eatock/Lafferty
" "	Stonecroft	
" "	Occupant	
House Name	John Fox Shirt (& Y.H.A. ?)	

Edale May Queen, 1933.

Right: *Shirt family members, Nether Booth, c.1920/30.*

TWO WORLD WARS

Booth	House Name	Occupant
Grindsbrook	Post Office and Farm	Percy and Jospeh Cooper
" "	Lea House and Farm	Arthur Rowbottom
" "	Western House	T. Tym/Robert Rodwell
" "	Wigley House	Allsop
" "	The Homestead	Lem Tym
" "	Sycamore Cottage	Mrs Lowe
" "	Corner Cottage	Mrs Charles
" "	Fold Head Cottage	Martha Cooper
" "	Fold Head	Jack and Kathleen Belfitt
" "	Homedene	Harold Rowbottom
" "	Homedene Annexe	George Slater/Steve Kay
" "	Nag's Head	Heardman
" "	Old Parsonage	Montague Brown
" "	The Lodge	Frank and Mrs Belfitt
" "	Grindslow House	Miss Champion
" "	The Warren	Georgie/Ivy/Phyllis Rowbottom
" "	Warren Cottage	Wright Dearnley
" "	Waterside Cottage	Grace Elliot/Jack and Amy Tym
" "	Hole (Brookside) Cottage	Burdekin
" "	Hole (Brookside) Cottage	Mrs Chapman, Grace and Florence
" "	Carr Bank Cottage	Bacon
" "	Carr Bank Cottage	Bentley
Ollerbrook	Ollerbrook Farm	James Thornley
" "	Middle Ollerbrook Farm	Vincent Fox
" "	Middle Ollerbrook Cottage	Woodcock
" "	Nether Ollerbrook Farm	Brown Bailey
" "	Nether Ollerbrook Cottage	Hamilton/J. Noblett
" "	Cotefield Farm	John Tym/Sarah Cooper
" "	Wood Farm (Springhill)	Shaws
" "	Wood House (Glan Noe)	Habersham/Greenstreets
Station to Mill and Back Tor Lane	Skinner's Hall Cottage	Les Eyre/John Eyre
" "	Skinner's Hall	Alf Harrison/Mrs Maudsley
" "	Hollins Farm	Wilsons
" "	Lower Hollins Farm	Vic Noblett
" "	18 Mill Cottages	Sweet/Bramley
" "	17 Mill Cottages	Harry Sims
" "	16 Mill Cottages	Arthur Lowe
" "	15 Mill Cottages	Eyres
" "	14 Mill Cottages	Harrops
" "	13 Mill Cottages	Vic Howe
" "	12 Mill Cottages	Mallinsons
" "	11 Mill Cottages	Wilf Hulse
" "	10 Mill Cottages	Geoff Noblett
" "	9 Mill Cottages	Smiths/Tym
" "	8 Mill Cottages	Arthur Dakin
" "	7 Mill Cottages	Mrs Bottom
" "	6 Mill Cottages	Elsie Tym
" "	5 Mill Cottages	Joe Marrison
" "	4 Mill Cottages	Arthur Tym/Ted Lowe
" "	3 Mill Cottages	Cowburns
" "	2 Mill Cottages	Atkinson
" "	1 Mill Cottages (?)	Hearnshaw
" "	Mill House	Povey
" "	Mill Lane Bungalow	Burrows
" "	Glen Tor	Mrs Harvey
" "	Ruskin Villa	Mrs Jackson/Miss Jones
" "	Peacehaven Bungalow	Hector Jackson
" "	Rose Cottage	Thomas Rowbottom
" "	Sunnyside Cottage	Fre Rowbottom
" "	Back Tor Farm	Goodwin/Dalton/Medley
Nether Booth	Rowland Cote	Batchelors
" "	Rowland Cottage	Ashfords
" "	Ladybooth Hall Farm	William Shirt
" "	Nether Booth Cottage	Arthur Mallinson
" "	Ladybooth Farm	Colin Tym/Elliot/Atkin
" "	Nether Booth Farm	Gilberts
" "	Clough Farm	Jack Elliot
" "	Carr Farm	Blackshaws
" "	Edale End Farm	Isaac Eyre
" "	Edale End	Tom Bridge

63

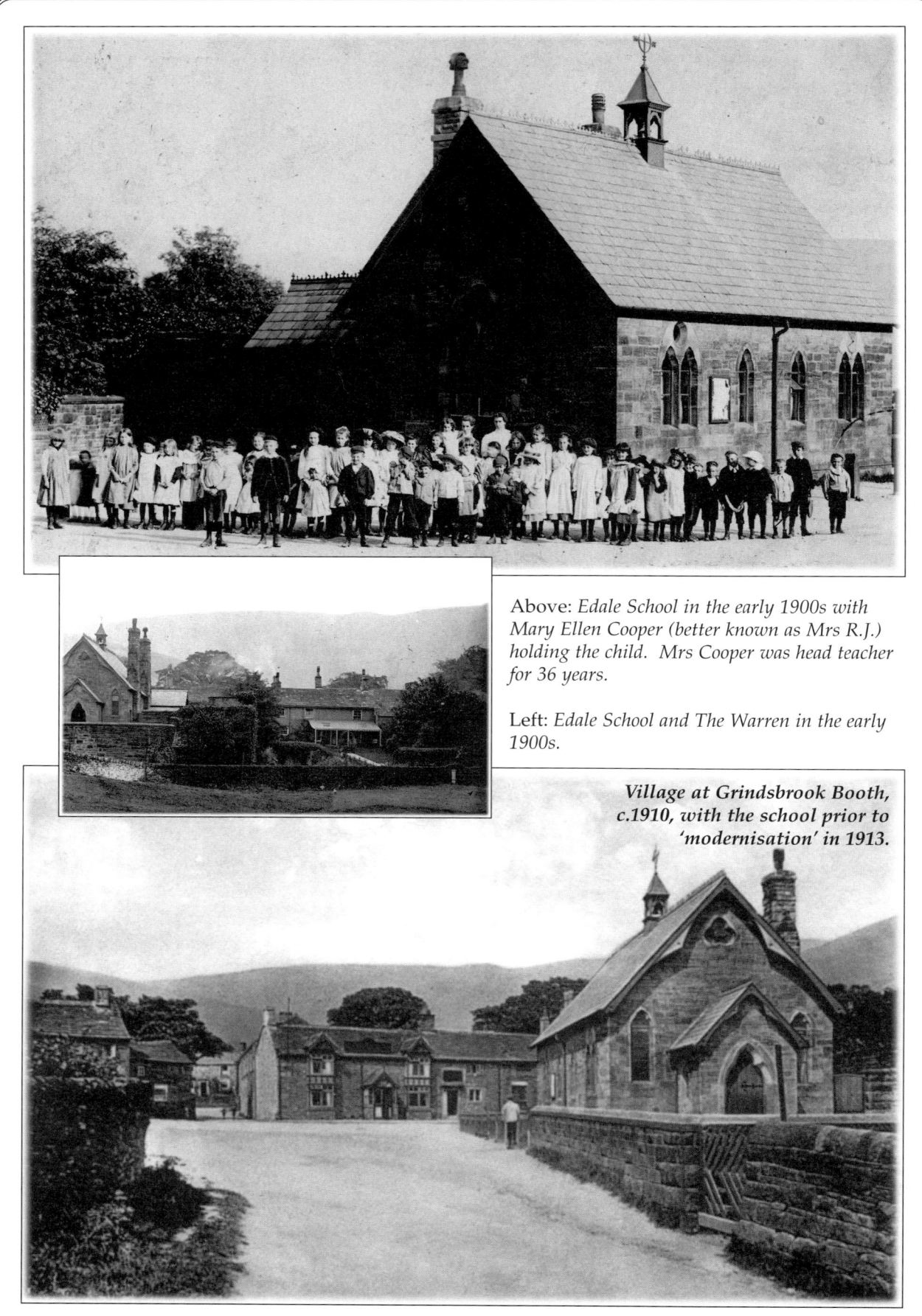

Above: *Edale School in the early 1900s with Mary Ellen Cooper (better known as Mrs R.J.) holding the child. Mrs Cooper was head teacher for 36 years.*

Left: *Edale School and The Warren in the early 1900s.*

Village at Grindsbrook Booth, c.1910, with the school prior to 'modernisation' in 1913.

Chapter Five

EDALE SCHOOL

The number of familiar faces in the school playground would strike anyone returning to Edale after being away from the village for many years. They would not know the children, but they would have known their parents and possibly their grandparents. And family likenesses in the valley are strong. Amongst the familiar faces they would also find lots of new faces, those of children whose families have moved into Edale more recently.

Edale School is in the centre of the settlement and in many ways the school is the heart of the village. Its value to the community is immense, a fact that is wholly appreciated by parents and other residents who work hard to support the school, both financially and in other ways.

Finding money for the village school is nothing new to Edale and energetic fund-raising helps keep it afloat. In the past, the school was also dependent on local benefactors.

THE SCHOOL'S BENEFACTORS

The first written record of education in Edale is related to a Joseph Tym, who died in 1708. Joseph donated annually the interest on £50 for teaching four poor children, the interest on £50 for poor inhabitants, and the interest on £50 for clothing poor women and children in linsey every St Thomas' Day.

In 1729 Revd Robert Turle contributed 40 shillings, the rent from his farm at Jack End in Hope parish, for the six poorest children to be taught to read English. These were to be nominated by the minister of Edale. A school was started by Thomas Cresswell in 1750 but there are no reports of its location. There is a report of a school in the grounds of the Old Parsonage, and those attending included an Issac Cooper. In 1784 Joseph Champion gave £70, half the interest of which was for the schoolmaster and the other half to buy penny loaves for the poor. The loaves were to be distributed after divine service on Sunday morning to those attending (unless too infirm or aged to attend).

The first real evidence of a permanent school is found in the establishment of the Elizabeth Bowden Trust. Prominent Edale residents, including the Champion family, were named as trustees. In 1819 Elizabeth Bowden granted to Charles Cecil Bates and others, including John Champion, two cottages and land amounting to six acres in Whitmore le Booth (now Barber Booth) and a plot of land in Grindsbrook Booth. The purpose of the trust was to permit Elizabeth Bowden and her heirs to erect a schoolhouse for teaching poor boys and girls reading, writing and arithmetic, together with a residence for a master. The school accounts had to be fixed to the door of the chapel on the Sunday after St John's Day. Seven poor children were to be taught free of charge. Some of the materials for building the school were to be brought from an older building used as a school, perhaps the Old Parsonage.

THE SCHOOL IN THE NINETEENTH CENTURY

Such was the beginning of the present Edale Church of England Primary School. Due to increasing demand the school was enlarged in 1868. 'Poor accommodation' lead to a 'modernisation' in 1913.

Edale School also played an important part in the social life of the village, providing a venue for village events right up to the building of the village hall in 1968. Although at some time another school had been established for the children of railway navvies between Barber Booth and Upper Booth in the early 1880s, the number of children in the village school continued to rise substantially.

Glimpses of the hardships and strictness of Victorian school life in a remote village school can be found in these extracts from the school diary:

Nov. 19th 1888 – Wet morning but fair attendance not withstanding 2 little girls E and A Bland, who live

Children outside school in the 1890s.

Schoolchildren, c.1890–1900.

Left: *Revd Adrian Murray-Leslie and school governor Gordon Miller replace the school bell in around 1995. The bell is used to summon the children from play. It was a tradition years ago for Bill Sims to ring in the New Year at the annual dance in the school.*

Below: *Edale schoolchildren in the church in 1911/12 with Annie Barnsley, infant teacher, far right.*

EDALE SCHOOL

Edale School, c.1913.

Edale schoolchildren about to embark on a trip to Blackpool in 1928. Left to right, back row: Harold Eyre, Archie Fletcher, Jack Ashmore, Jim Smith, Douglas Hawtin, Frank Wilson, George Mallinson; third row: Mrs M.E. Cooper (Mrs R.J.) headmistress, Ruth Tym, May Kirkby, Edna Mallinson, Kathleen Wilson, Irene Blow, Eva Shirt, Ivy Rowbottom, Hilda Fletcher, Barbara Lloyd; second row: Margaret Smith, Cynthia Poulson, Phoebe Scholey, Lily Mallinson, Joan Sweet, Gladys Mallinson, Amy Tym, Margaret Harvey, Dora Sims, Mary Shepherd; front row: Arnold Fletcher, Noel Davies, Frank Tym, Joseph Shepherd, Peter Burrows, George Goodwin, Eric Hulme, Billy Smith.

Edale School, 1929. Left to right, back row: Joseph Shepherd, George Mallinson, Frank Wilson, Arthur Cooper, Jack Smith, Douglas Hawtin, Arnold Fletcher, John Eyre; third row: Jack Ashmore or Smith, Ivy Rowbottom, Irene Blow, Alice Harrop, Eva Shirt, George Goodwin, Mrs R.J. Cooper (head teacher); second row: Edna Mallinson, Margaret Rowbottom, Jean Rowbottom, Ruth Tym, Barbara Lloyd, Mary Shepherd, Margaret Harvey, May Kirkby, Kathleen Wilson; front row: Billy Smith, Noel Davies, Howard Eyre, Frank Tym, Peter Boroughs.

Edale School, c.1930. Left to right, back row: Frank Tym, Geoff Critchlow, John Tym, ?, Noel Davies, Thomas Maudsley, Geoff Hawtin, Ted Lowe; third row: Joan Sweet, Amy Tym, Phoebe Scholey, Ruth Tym, Margaret Smith, Margaret Thornley, Margaret Rowbottom, Hazel Jackson, Dora Sims; second row: Doreen Gilbert, ?, Ros Rowbottom, Brenda Wilson, Rosamund Burdikin, Lilian Cooper, ?, ?, Miss Dawson (teacher); front row: Frank Tym, Brian Lloyd, Arthur Marrison, George Dakin, Brian Cooper, John Tym, Reg Hawtin, John Rowbottom.

EDALE SCHOOL

about 3 miles from school, went home at 3.00pm to allow for getting home before dark

June 10th 1889 – Mrs A. Rowbottom appointed as Sewing Mistress

July 1889 – Jan and Harriet Evans arrive just after time for marking the register – have marked absent

July 4th 1889 – Many children absent because of the hay harvest

August 1889 – 46 children present at school. Mrs Champion of Grindslow House [a trustee] was a regular visitor to inspect needlework.

Sept 23rd 1889 – 59 children present

Feb 1890 – Chin cough has spread to many families

June 26th 1890 – Extremely wet morning, only 6 children in school

Dec 12th 1890 – Damp, foggy weather has prevented attendance by many – am obliged to get the children close to the fire to keep themselves warm

Aug 27th 1891 – Managers agreed to accept fee grant – no fees to be charged after Sept 1st 1891

Sept 5th 1891 – Attendance low as many children have gone with their parents to Hope Agricultural Show or Castleton Wakes

May 21st–28th 1894 – A weeks holiday for Edale Wakes

May 18th 1900 – Holiday for Queen Victoria's birthday and the Relief of Mafeking

By 1904 there were 224 adults in Edale and 83 children under 14 years old, the age at which they left the school. The school managers that year recommended that the piano be removed from the school, and that the fireplaces be improved. Two locals, Harold Rowbottom and Margaret E. Cooper, were to become student teachers at the school. In 1909 discussions began about enlarging the school and an estimate of £600 was given. The salary of a new assistant teacher was set at £35 per annum, while Martha Cooper was appointed caretaker at a salary of £8 per annum. Financial support for the enlargement was sought from the Midland Railway Company (in respect of the children of railway servants) and from Fine Cotton Spinners who owned Edale Mill. The school was finally enlarged in 1913 at an actual cost of £1081.18s.

Dates in the School Calender

In 1930 Mary Ellen Cooper (née Barber), known locally as 'Mrs R.J.', ended 36 years' service as the headmistress on 19 December. In 1932 Edna Mallinson and Betty Kirkland started as probationary teachers. The following year the school was closed for a day on 21 July for the funeral of a young pupil, George Goodwin, killed tragically while cycling home from school.

On 3 September 1939 the outbreak of war was announced and the school did not reassemble until 13 September, by which time the numbers on the roll had risen dramatically with the arrival of 27 children and two teachers evacuated from Oswald Road Municipal School in Manchester. The large numbers in the school meant a shift system for teaching, and Cooper's Café across the road became the school annexe.

At one time a shortage of coke for the boiler meant that all classes were held in the infants' room, so all the pupils could get near the coal fire. Records show that five pairs of wellingtons were issued to Roy Cooper, Peter Noblett, Ann Noblett, June Corrigan and Ronald Corrigan, while other children later received supplementary clothing coupons.

In 1933 the school was caught up in a village controversy when the vicar banned plays by Edale's dramatic society from being performed in the school, and the school managers required that 'all plays, sketches and operettas to be performed in school be submitted for approval.' A note from the Education Board in the school minutes records this as an illegal act! (There is more about this episode in the school's history in Chapter Eight.)

In 1944 the first school dinners were provided and were taken in Cooper's Café until a kitchen was built in the school in 1959. That same year the playground was surfaced with tarmac. A youth club was formed in 1947 and requested the use of the school for meetings. In 1968, when HRH Princess Margaret visited Edale, the schoolchildren sang in the church.

A site for a new school was agreed with the National Park planners in 1971 but its development was 'not likely to be for many years!' Since then the number of pupils has dwindled considerably. On one occasion the school was threatened with closure because of the low number of pupils. However, the indomitable spirit of the Edale villagers raised thousands of pounds to safeguard the school's future. One of the major fund-raising activities is the now-ever-popular Edale Country Day that attracts visitors from near and far.

Since 1846 the head teachers at the school have been as follows:

1846–62	*John Bardsley*
1862–76	*William Hamer*
1876–81	*A. Turner*
1881–83	*William Jervis Jackson*
1883–94	*William Naylor*
1894–1930	*Mary E. Cooper*
1931	*Amy Borrow*
1931–35	*Doris Dawson*
1935–40	*Ivy Waite*
1940–43	*O.M. Coleman*
1943–49	*Hannah Harvey*
1949–74	*F.E. Ellacott*
1975–85	*Bettine Barker*
1985–91	*Des Hoskisson*
1991–98	*Peter Irwin*
1998–	*Sandra Pillans*

Edale School in 1930. Left to right, back row: Thomas Maudsley, Margaret Thornley, ?, Ted Hawtin, John Tym, ?; middle row: Margaret Rowbottom, Margaret Dakin, Geoff Critchlow, John Rowbottom, Roy Scott, Alan Tym, Lilian Cooper, Hazel Jackson, Dora Sims; front row: ?, Reg Hawtin, ?, Ted Lowe.

Edale School, 1931. Left to right, back row: Miss Abbott, Arthur Marrison, Reg Martin, Geoffrey Critchlow, Ted Lowe, Clifford Cooper, George Dakin; middle row: Beryl Howe, Phyllis Wilson, Margaret Gregory, Dora Sims, Lilian Cooper, Rosmund Rowbottom, ?, Rosamund Burdikin; front row: John Rowbottom, Jean Martin, Maurice Tym, ?, Margaret Dakin, Norah Rowbottom, Doreen Gilbert, Gordon Cooper.

EDALE SCHOOL

Edale School, 1933/4. Pictured are head teacher Miss Waite (front right) with infant teacher Miss Abbott behind.

Edale School, c.1934. Left to right, back row: Tony Jackson, Harry Dakin, Geo Goodwin, Ron Hunter, Alf Haggert, Jim Thornley, Billy Kermode; third row: Norman Hunter, Pat Gilbert, Jean Smith, Joan Bidwell, Sheila Scholey, ? Tyson, ?, ?, Eric Hunter; second row: Billy Hulse, Jill Tillott, Brenda Foster, ?, Monica Gilbert, Peggy Smith; front row: Austin Broadbent, Joe Mallinson, ? Haggert, John Lowe, ?, Des Howe.

THE BOOK OF EDALE

Left: *Edale School in the 1950s with head teacher Mrs Ellacott.*

Right: *Edale School trip to Chester in 1954.*

Left: *Edale School, 1961.*

EDALE SCHOOL

Edale School in around 1960. Left to right, back row: John Shirt, Peter Atkin, Julian Mullins, Elizabeth Rodwell, R. Jefferies, David Chapman; front row: Alan Tym, Gail Angus, ?, ?, P. Rowbottom.

Edale School in 1961, winners of the Hope Valley Athletics Shield. Left to right: Margaret Hornsby, Trevor Bowler, David Chapman, ?, Walter Carnall, John Shirt, Peter Atkin, Julian Mullins, Elizabeth Rodwell.

Edale School, c.1962.

Edale School, c.1962/3. Left to right, back row: K. Wilkinson, A. Tym, B. Goodwin, S. Reid, P. Beney, J. Atkin, M. Yeardley; front row: D. Shirt, K. Beney, M. Carnall, G. Garlick, P. Atkin, G. Wilkinson.

EDALE SCHOOL

Edale School, 1977.

Left: *Following the fitting of kitchen facilities, children take their dinners in school for the first time in 1961. Previously they had crossed the road to Cooper's Café.*

Edale School, 1982.

Above: *Edale School, 1985. Left to right, back row: Miss Amy Tym, Mrs Ruby Hunter, Katy Nichols, Gillian Nield, Diane Shirt, Esther Holdsworth, Laura Rennison, Hannah Murray-Leslie, Lucinda Coghlan, Mrs Sandra Pillans (infants' teacher), Mrs Bettine Barker (head teacher); third row: Andrew Hill, Michelle Allen, Jonathan Gilbert, Michael Wilson, Gawain Murray-Leslie, Dean Sowerby, Ian Cooper, James Metcalfe; second row: Mrs Rene Wilkinson, Marina Odom, Milly Holdsworth, Rebecca Murray-Leslie, Pauline Shirt, Rebecca Naylor, Naomi Miller, Ellen Naylor, Mrs Judy Dean; front row: Rupert Holdsworth, Paul Cooper, Alistair Metcalfe, Russell Odom, David Shirt, David Naylor.*

Below: *Infants' teacher Mary McVeigh (with white headband) and Edale schoolchildren take a rest during a walk in Grindsbrook, 1991.*

Above: *Edale School football team, Hope Wakes Trophy winners in 2001. Left to right, back row: Daniel Wallington, David Raw, Annie Wheeler, front row: Francis Wallington, Richard Worthington, Oliver Mount, Peter Whittaker, Matthew Hemsley (captain).*

EDALE SCHOOL

Left: *Edale School, 1993. Left to right, back row: Peter Irwin (head teacher), Julia Yeardley, James Butcher, Bella Hardy, Christopher Reid, Rachel Gee, Claire Yeardley, Mary McVeigh (infants' teacher); middle row: Catherine Reid, Sarah Gee, Heather Shirt, Laura Skillen, Joanna Reid, Abigail Metcalfe, Sarah Willsmer; front row: Rosie McSheehy, Katy Whittaker, Alex Hemsley, Laura McSheehy, Tom Searle, Georgina Wheeler, Lee Willsmer, Amy Mount.*

Right: *Edale schoolchildren picnic on the slopes of Kinder in 1992.*

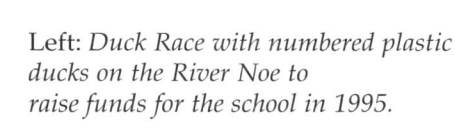

Left: *Duck Race with numbered plastic ducks on the River Noe to raise funds for the school in 1995.*

Edale School, 1995. Left to right, back row: Lyn Elliott (infants' teacher), Amy Mount, Peter Irwin (head teacher), Lee Willsmer, Philip ?, Francis Wallington, Katy Whittaker, ? (visitor); middle row: Georgina Wheeler, Laura McSheehy, Rachel Gee, Abigail Metcalfe, Claire Yeardley, Elizabeth Archer, Sarah Willsmer, Alex Hemsley; front row: Peter Whittaker, Rosie McSheehy, Richard Worthington, Tom Searle, Annie Wheeler, Matthew Hemsley, Alice Mount.

Edale Church with the southern edges of Kinder. The stone for the building of the church was quarried from Nether Tor, the rock outcrop behind the spire. The stone was dragged down the hillside by horse-drawn sleds creating channels which are still visible.

Left: *The entrance to the Parish Church of the Holy and Undivided Trinity at Edale.*

Chapter Six

CHURCH AND CHAPEL

For many visitors to Edale, one of the enduring memories they take home is the sight of the church spire towering against the hills that are the start of the Pennine Way. Equally picturesque is the Methodist chapel, tucked away among the trees at Barber Booth. But there is far more to the story than pretty buildings. Who could guess from these idyllic scenes that Methodism in Edale started in a humble cottage, long since disappeared, on a site next to where the chapel stands at the time of writing? Or that a family bereavement in the early-seventeenth century meant carrying a coffin for three miles over the hilltops to be buried in another village?

EDALE CHURCH

The church standing in 2003 is the third to be built in Edale. On the opposite side of the road to the existing church can be seen an older graveyard with the original stone font still standing within its walls. This was the site of the first chapel, built in 1633 and consecrated in 1634 by the Bishop of Coventry and Lichfield. There were 15 co-founders: Robert Hall, Stephen Bright, Thomas Hall, Robert Carrington, Frances Howe, Henry Hall, George Howe, Gyles Barber, Thomas Barber, Ralph Cresswell, John Hadfield, Roger Hall, George Lowe, Anna Shore and Alice Carrington. Their duties were to help maintain the fabric of the church, nominate the minister, and pay him £10 per year. This duty devolved to their heirs.

Over the years the condition of this first chapel deteriorated and it became too small for all those wishing to attend services. Application was made to dismantle the structure and the cost of rebuilding it entirely was estimated by a Mr John Bishop, architect, at £1,480.18s.4d. This first appeal to rebuild the chapel met with little success, and it was not until 1808 that another, more successful, appeal was made and the building of the second chapel began. The structure was simple as can be seen from the engraving below, and over the door was placed the inscription 'Edale chapel originally built AD MDCXXXIII (1633) was taken down and replaced by this present edifice AD MDCCCXII (1812).'

THE COFFIN ROUTE

Before the building of the first chapel in 1633, the people of Edale attended Castleton Church. This involved a steep, sometimes perilous, journey over the ridge at Hollins Cross, more than 1,200 feet above sea level. When they reached Castleton, worshippers followed a narrow passageway between the shops and into the church by a side entrance. Coffins had to be carried the three miles, whatever the weather. Most of the old coffin route can still be walked and it is a popular path between the two villages.

Architect's drawing for the new church built in 1885. The chapel, which it replaced, is also shown. The chapel stood on the site of the old graveyard. The old Church Inn can be seen on the far left in the drawing.

A NEW PARISH AND A NEW CHURCH

On 9 January 1863 Edale became a separate parish and the event was recorded in the *London Gazette*. The church which is in existence at the time of writing was built in 1885, just across the road from the two earlier chapels. A committee was formed to help raise funds. Members were: Joseph Taylor, W. Champion, A. Jowitt, F. Thornley, William Burdikin, A. Gee, Richard Cooper, Mrs Champion and Revd F. Champion, vicar.

A contemporary description of the church mentions the nave and chancel with '222 sittings, all

THE BOOK OF EDALE

Below: *Footpath to the church from Ollerbrook, c.1930.*

Above: *The Parish Church of the Holy and Undivided Trinity in Edale. The church was built in 1885 and the tower added four years later.*

Right: *The interior of Edale Holy Trinity Church.*

CHURCH AND CHAPEL

Micah Tym's funeral card, 1909.

free, and also the Vestry and the Tower to height of 240 feet.' Most of this had been paid for, but funds were still required to complete the tower and spire. These were not immediately forthcoming, and the building (by an Alfred Hill of Litton) did not begin until four years later.

The new churchyard of one acre was given by 'F. Thornley Esq' but a stone wall was needed to enclose this before it would be suitable for burials. The cost of this outstanding work was estimated to be £747, and more subscriptions were sought.

The foundation-stone was laid by Lord Edward Cavendish, the Duke of Devonshire's son. The builder was Thomas Beck of Matlock Bridge, and stone for the construction was brought down the hillside from Nether Tor, a gritstone outcrop overlooking the Grindsbrook Valley. The new church was named the Church of the Holy and Undivided Trinity, and it was consecrated by the Bishop of Southwell on 26 June 1886.

Fittingly for Edale, there was a heavy downpour during the ceremony. However, the Nether Tor stone survived the weather, and has endured to this day. Some of the fittings and adornments from the old chapel can be seen in the church at the time of writing. These include brasses and tablets, and a panel that once hung above the communion table and which is now set in the chancel wall.

Church Upkeep and Maintenance

Fund-raising is, and always has been, an important issue for most churches. Edale is no exception. The church accounts for the year ending 30 April 1896 give some idea of life at that time. Among special funds set aside from church collections were £1.6s.0d. for the 'Sick and poor', collected at Whitsun; £1.5s.8d. for the Church of England Temperance Society; and an Easter collection of £2.2s.3d. for church improvements. The organist's salary was £5 and the organ blower received 10 shillings. Sacramental wine came to three shillings, and the washing of surplices, two shillings. A new bell rope cost 4s.6d. The Edale church tower repair fund collected over £16.

The latter item reflects contemporary concerns, when funds are still being sought to repair the church spire – a problem probably not helped by those Edale downpours and by the number of jackdaws who have made their homes in the spire.

The Methodist Chapel

Edale Methodist Chapel is in a secluded spot at Barber Booth, next door to the small cottage where Methodism first began in Edale.

In 1750 David Taylor and a companion were travelling through the hills from Sheffield to Sparrowpit (where he had started a Methodist society in 1738) when they were caught in a blinding snowstorm. Fatigued and almost perishing they reached the cottage at Barber Booth and sought shelter.

The good man of the house, John Hadfield, thinking the visitors were influenced by evil, reached down his sword, which hung over the mantelpiece alongside the other armour he had used at the Battle of Preston Pans a few years before. But his fears were soon dispelled when David Taylor stepped up to him and said 'Peace be to this house.'

Methodist services in Edale started from that time and a society was formed, of which John Hadfield was the first member. In the same cottage James Ridal, a travelling preacher, was born, and a farmstead across the valley was the birthplace of Daniel and Peter Eyre, both of whom became Wesleyan ministers.

From these beginnings the chapel was built in 1811. The Sunday school seems to have been added at the end of the century. There were two chapel services, afternoon and evening, every Sunday. In 2003 there is only an afternoon service, held twice a month.

Percival Harvey was the Sunday school leader, from about 1930–45, and classes were held in the afternoon before the service. There was also a regular choir. Horace and Bessie Dalton continued to lead the Sunday school when they came to live at Back Tor and later at Ladybooth Farm. Some years later a Sunday school was held in the village hall. It became too expensive for those who attended, the chapel Sunday school was 'done up' and sessions were held there.

In 2003 only a few members attend the chapel, but it is well loved and cared for and at harvest festival and Christmas is often full.

For many years the chapel and Sunday school were centrally heated by a coke-burning boiler in the

Edale Holy Trinity Church from the old graveyard, site of the earlier chapel.

81

Above: *The Methodist chapel and adjoining Sunday school, Barber Booth.*

Right: *Edale Mothers' Union charter, 1948.*

Below: *Edale Mothers' Union by the War Memorial at Edale Church at the dedication of the banner. Mrs Esme Hornsby (standing between the Bishop of Derby and the banner) made the banner and later lead local women in producing tapestry kneelers for the church. The churchwarden Mr Wright Dearnley is on the far left and the vicar, Revd C.S. Rawlinson, is on the far right. Also included in the photograph are: Mrs J. Thornley, Mrs A. Rowbottom, Edith Burdikin, Mrs Lem Tym and Mrs Bentley.*

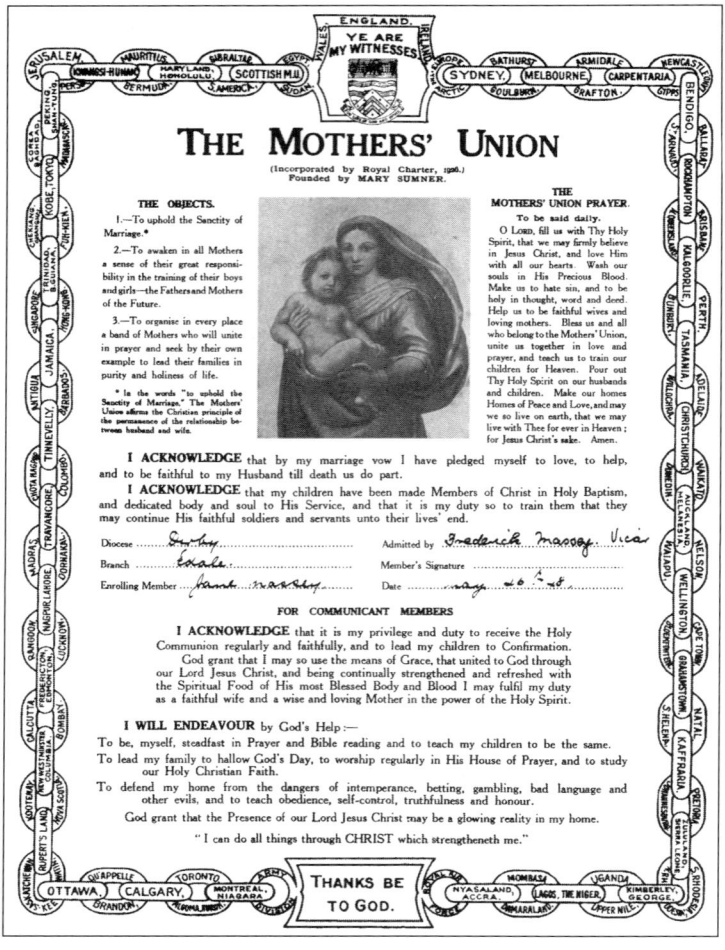

CHURCH AND CHAPEL

Above: Inhabitants of Edale pose for a photograph to celebrate the church centenary in 1985. Left to right, back row: Liz Gilbert, Penny Townsend, David Howe, Ian Widowson, Carol Jefferson-Davis, Ruth and Lawrence Yeardley, John Atkin, Cedric Gilbert, Jane Hodgson, Mandy Oakes, Sheila Cooper, Kenny Baker, Rosemary McKeon, Peter Cooper, Sue Mitchell, Edwin Townsend, David Naylor, David Wilson, Oliver and Robin Metcalfe, Jo Falzon, Dave and Trevor Teare, Charlie Falzon, Alan Chapman, Belinda Critchlow, Michael Holdsworth, Derek Sowerby, Val Gilbert, Lynda Shirt, Stan Hodgson, Tony Favell, Colin Odom, Jeremy Blunden, Amanda Blunden, Victoria McKeon, Andrew Critchlow, David Baird, Vic Archer, Andrew Wilson, Jeanne Tucker, Margaret Dolly, Alan Tym, Magda Rennison, John Tupholme, David Shirt, John Blunden, Caroline Jackson, Tricia and Adrian Murray-Leslie; third row: Clive and Elizabeth Wetherall, Wendy and James Butcher, Bill Smith, Rosalyn, Glenys and John Nield, Shirley and Stuart Chapman, Tony Gilbert, David Worthington, Robert Davis, Amanda and Chris Cowan, Josie and Des Howe, Gordon and Denise Miller, Harry and Joan Newton, Geoff Critchlow, Jean Chapman, Barbara Neves, Amy Tym, Jane Beney, Margaret Wheeler, Stephen and Annabel Coghlan, Eileen Wright, Bob Townsend, Richard and Linda Nicholson, Julia Emery, Kathryn Reid, Mrs Gilbert, Dorothy Baird, Nora and John Earl, Mark, Christine, Sue, Alison and Dick Baxter, Ann Blunden, Judith Shirt, Betty Miles-Ward, Sue Favell, Norah McKeon, Barbara Worthington; second row: Helen Nicholson, Milly Heardman, Vic Noblett, Pauline and Horace Jackson, Muriel Shirt, Jean Rodwell, John, Rachael, Sarah and Sally Gee, Joyce Elliott, George and Reta Mullins, Audrey and Jim Shirt, Ted Wright, James Cooper, Tom Nield, Frank Wilson, Martha Tym, Gladys Lowe, Jane and Elizabeth Archer, Marion and Eleanor Odom, Florence Allsop, Grace Kay, Vera Goodwin, Hannah Roberts, Jim and Edith Carrington, Doris Reid holding Joanna Reid, Maggy Prior, Charles and Joan Williams, Edna Wright, Pattie Harrison, Frances Steer, Margaret and Pat Wrenn holding Alex Odom, Dorothy Smith, Betty Walker, Sue Townsend; front row: Tania Wetherall, Gavain, Hannah and Rebecca Murray-Leslie, Beryl Townsend holding Louise Townsend, Michelle Allan, Jessica Wetherall, Rosie and Andrew Favell, Simon Jackson, Luke Archer, Alistair and James Metcalfe, Russell Odon, Janet, Sally and Helen Atkin, Julie Sowerby, Louisa Nicholson, Dean Sowerby, Morgan Jackson, Raymond Critchlow, Jason Nicholson, Esther Holdsworth, Naomi Miller, Jennie Holdsworth holding Millicent Holdsworth, Lindsey Gilbert, Livia and Rupert Holdsworth, Holdsworth cousins, Judith Davis, Charles Coghlan, Danny Tym, Michael Wilson, Sophie and Lucinda Coghlan, Gillian Nield, Michelle Townsend, Katie Butcher, Marina Odom, Lara Rennison, Diane and Heather Shirt, Pauline Shirt, David Shirt, Anne Worthington holding two children.

Right: Edale Church Centenary, 1985. Local children Diane Shirt, Becky Murray-Leslie, Naomi Miller and Raymond Critchlow build a model church during the celebrations at the Village Hall Field.

83

cellar, which was lit and stoked by the caretakers Mr and Mrs Tom Nield. This was done every Saturday from the early 1930s until the late 1940s when the boiler blew up. After this the only means of heating were paraffin heaters plus an open fire in the Sunday school. Electricity arrived in the dale in 1951, after which time heating the chapel was easier and safer. Mr and Mrs Nield were caretakers from 1933 until the late 1950s.

The Peak Centre at Champion House

Champion House is a residential youth centre which was set up in the heart of Edale in the 1960s. It was first thought of as a way of offering an alternative experience to city youngsters and is run jointly by the Diocese of Derby and Derbyshire County Council Youth Service. It accommodates 20 young people and four leaders.

The centre was made possible by the donation of a barn standing next to the vicarage garden by Mrs Caroline Noel of Grindslow House. Mrs Noel is a descendant of Revd John Champion, hence the name of the centre. The barn was developed to include a dormitory and toilet wing. It was opened by the Bishop of Derby and is supervised by the resident vicar. Princess Margaret visited Champion House in June 1969, when Revd Michael Bishop was the first full-time warden. The Princess had tea in the village hall before making her way to Champion House and Fieldhead Information Centre. This was followed by a short service in the church.

At the time of writing the Peak Centre is a busy activity centre with a climbing wall and facilities for archery and outdoor pursuits. Young people coming to Edale for the first time can enjoy a complete change from city life, get to know the countryside, and discover their own abilities. The centre is also used by the villagers for group celebrations and talks.

In 2002 it was decided to change the name of the centre and Champion House became The Peak Centre at Champion House.

Above left: *The Methodist chapel at Barber Booth before the building of the Sunday school annexe.*

Above right: *Chapel-goers outside the Methodist chapel at Barber Booth.*

Left: *The Sunday school outside the Nag's Head Inn, 1916.*

CHURCH AND CHAPEL

Champion House with the original old barn donated by the Champion family and converted to the first residential centre.

Above: *HRH Princess Margaret at the opening of Champion House.*

Above: *The Duke of Devonshire, HRH Princess Margaret and Revd Michael Bishop leave the vicarage during the visit to Edale when they visited the church, Champion House Diocesan Outdoor Centre and the National Park Information Centre.*

Left: *Champion House with modern additions.*

Tourist postcard of Edale, 1961.

Below: *A group of walkers in 1939 outside a shooting cabin below Nether Tor, Grindsbrook, which is now in ruins. The walker on the far left is Mr Campie Barrows, who later became a voluntary warden for the National Park.*

Rowland Cote, now Edale Youth Hostel.

Chapter Seven

RECREATION

Edale has long been the spiritual home for those who seek tranquillity or excitement, solitude or the companionship of like-minded fell walkers. Heather, bilberry and crowberry, rocky streams and groughs, skylarks, golden plover and grouse all form part of the rich mosaic of the dark gritstone peat bogs that encircle Edale.

The wilderness and rugged terrain of Kinder Scout has always attracted walkers, scramblers and climbers to the Edale area. This attraction was sometimes spiced with excitement because, until 1932, access to the open moorland was 'unofficial'. In that year the Ramblers' Association staged a mass trespass on Kinder – an event that marked the beginning of open access to the moors for everyone.

ESCAPE FROM THE CITIES

Working-class people from Manchester and Sheffield, short on leisure time and low on income, were able to access the area more easily after the opening of the railway from Manchester to Sheffield in 1898. The hills became so important to these people that members of the Clarion Club in Sheffield purchased part of Losehill – between Edale, Hope and Castleton – in memory of one of their members, Joseph Ward. This land is called Ward's Piece and is open to the general public.

Cyclists too, often with little money but a lot of spirit and determination, came to Edale seeking fresh air, freedom and wildlife. Members of the Cyclist Touring Club found the old packhorse routes ideal for reaching the high moors above the village. Jacob's Ladder originally led the jaggers and their strings of ponies up to Edale Cross and over to Hayfield and Glossop. Now, after crossing the River Noe on the delightful arched packhorse bridge beyond Upper Booth, it is cyclists who toil their way to the top of Jacob's Ladder. Even today, on technically superior mountain bikes, this is still a challenging way to leave Edale.

Joining the walkers and cyclists on the often-hazardous road over Mam Nick into Edale are motor cars, which were becoming increasingly affordable during the 1930s and 1940s. In fact, the Simplex Car Company in Sheffield tested their cars on the local hills. For young people, motorbikes offered a similar and less expensive means of getting around. Today the fields below Back Tor are used once a year to host a motorbike scramble – an event that never fails to take walkers on the Losehill Ridge by surprise.

Increasingly, Edale came to represent freedom – from the city, from the mills and factories and from the confines of the industrial regime. On the moors and along the valley paths people could forget about the factory clock, the rigid shift patterns and the timetables. In Edale, clocking on and off was not required. Camp-sites, such as those at Cooper's and Fieldhead, and the conversion of the old Batchelor family home at Rowland Cote in the 1940s to a youth

The Cooper's camp-site in the early 1960s.

A group of villagers enjoy a break during a cycle ride to the Derwent Valley in 1985.

The interior of the first Cooper's Café. The building was constructed from two former railway carriages. For some time it was both a café and a briefing centre for voluntary National Park wardens and was a welcome stop for walkers wanting a good mug of tea.

hostel, helped to provide cheaper accommodation for those on low or non-existent wages.

Before it became a National Park Visitor Centre, camp-site and ranger base, the farmhouse at Fieldhead was run during the early 1940s by Mr and Mrs Pemberton as a guest-house. The 15 guests all shared one bathroom, a situation that would not be tolerated today in the bed-and-breakfast establishments in the village! Meals, which were simple but adequate, were taken in a building next to the farmhouse.

Winter Sports

If walking and cycling provided a cheap, simple form of escapism, activities in winter became rather more 'Continental'. Before the demolition of the mill-dam on the River Noe in the 1930s, Fred Heardman could be seen leaping and twirling about on the frozen millpond, ice-skates on his feet instead of the more familiar bog-trotting boots. Even more popular amongst locals and visitors was the sport of skiing. Along with sledges and toboggans, skis were frequently needed when transporting people, supplies or even animals during the often harsh winters of the Edale Valley and moors.

Pat Atkin, at Nether Booth (Lady Booth), remembers Brenda Smith, who ran the Church Hotel from 1945 until 1972, hiring skis out to visitors and locals, even before the ski tow was set up in 1970. After a day on the slopes, the skiers would sit in the Church Hotel, their skis and boots drying out on the fender around the fire, leaving pools of melting snow.

The setting up of a ski tow above the field behind Lea Barn by Peat Lane was popular with residents and also brought many visiting skiers into the village. Cars would drive up to the village square to park as close as possible to the ski-run.

Many of today's full-time and part-time rangers remember hectic, and often hazardous, times on the ski tow. Tobogganists as well as skiers flew down the slopes. And it was not only people who went hurtling by! Sometimes pieces of machinery from the tow itself whizzed down the hill. Rangers were kept busy, separating colliding sledges and skis, and occasionally tending to broken bones and other injuries. Chaos often ensued in the village square, as drivers tried to cram their vehicles into the restricted space, and rangers doubled up as traffic wardens. The closure of the ski tow in the 1970s was followed by the milder winters of the twentieth century, when conditions became less severe; nowadays the little snow we do have does not lie on the ground for long.

Ice-skating and skiing may have declined in popularity, but the old packhorse routes are enjoying a new-found favour. Following in the 'hooves' of their ancestors, today's ponies carry a different load. Visitors and local people now go pony-trekking and horse riding. The trekking centre at Nether Booth (Lady Booth) has been firmly established since 1962. Bridle-ways from Edale pass over the moors to the Derwent, Hayfield, Glossop, and Peak Forest, and a new long-distance bridle-way route is being created at the time of writing.

Edale Valley in winter.

Fred Heardman skating on the pond at Edale Mill, 1933.

RECREATION

The ski-run above Grindsbrook Booth in around 1968.

Left: *Alice Cooper and Helen Heardman outside the Post Office around 1947. Mrs Heardman, a midwife and pioneer of natural childbirth, played a prominent part in the Kinder Players and various drama productions in the Hope Valley.*

Above: *Icicles in Grindsbrook.*

Left: *A winter scene at Grindsbrook.*

89

Above: *Elizabeth* (left), *Lindsay Gilbert* (right) *and friends riding above the Edale Valley, 1980.*

Right: *Pony trekkers leave Ladybooth Farm at Nether Booth on an excursion into the surrounding hills.*

A paraglider landing in an Edale meadow in 2002. Mam Tor, above the village, attracts hang-glider and parascender enthusiasts from all over the world.

RECREATION

Meanwhile, up in the air, paragliders, parascenders and hang-gliders defy gravity as they hover and swoop above the valley. Freed from earthly constraints, these gaily-coloured pieces of confetti can be seen over Mam Tor, Rushup Edge and Dale Head, when atmospheric conditions permit. On the ground they are less graceful, and the 'pilots' look like ants struggling under the burdens of their enormous packs. Landings can sometimes be painful and occasionally the mountain-rescue team is called in to help.

THE PENNINE WAY

Walking on the moors and in the valley has always been, and probably always will be, the most popular recreational pastime for visitors to Edale. Part of the attraction is the Pennine Way, Britain's first long-distance national trail. Finally opened in 1965, this challenging route starts from the village square outside the Nag's Head and, for 268 miles, winds its way along the Pennines to Kirk Yetholm in Scotland. It crosses terrain so challenging that the famous Alfred Wainwright, fell walker and author of many guides, vowed never to return to certain areas of the Dark Peak again, and this was on the second day of the route!

Many books and programmes have been written or recorded about this fascinating route. As a young Area Ranger, Gordon Miller had an entertaining time with John Noakes and his well-known dog Shep when the duo from 'Blue Peter' were filmed walking the Pennine Way. Being a studio dog, Shep was not used to long-distance walking and, after going AWOL, was found asleep behind a peat grough! Another famous dog on the Way was Boogie, who featured in the Edale author's book *Long Distance Walkies with Boogie*. Mark Wallington, living and writing in Edale, completed the distance, as did Boogie. But it was far more of a challenge than they had bargained for.

In fact, walkers have always underestimated the Pennine Way, and the start (or finish) from Edale is notoriously treacherous. Deep, dark peat bogs, low clouds and swirling mists, and an infinite number of maze-like groughs, conspire to confuse and exhaust the novice walker. The early wardens were kept busy advising, searching for and rescuing lost and injured Pennine wayfarers, a tradition continued today by current rangers and mountain-rescue teams from Edale, Hayfield and Buxton. Many a copy of Wainwright's guide ended up in the dustbin after an exciting encounter with the vagaries of Kinder Scout, including that once owned by the Area Ranger at the time of writing when she was a young teenager!

MOORLAND ACCESS

The Depression years of the 1930s brought enforced leisure time to masses of people living in the industrial cities bordering the Peak District, and the promise of fresh air and open spaces encouraged many to forsake their home surroundings and to venture into the hills. However, the open moorland, with the exception of a few rights of way, was out of bounds because they were grouse-shooting moors and access was by permit only. Mass meetings of ramblers were held in the Winnats Pass and Cave Dale in Castleton, and were addressed by politicians and activists demanding free access to the open moorland.

These meetings provided an opportunity for frustrated ramblers to voice their opinions, but for others a more proactive approach was to lead to the now-famous Mass Trespass on the Kinder Scout plateau. On Sunday 24 April 1932, walkers assembled at Hayfield to walk on to Kinder where they were joined by other walkers from Sheffield who had climbed up from Edale. The ensuing skirmishes resulted in six youths being imprisoned. Further mass meetings in the Winnats Pass and at Jacob's Ladder in Edale were to influence the establishment of the Peak District as Britain's first National Park in 1951 and the start of negotiations for legal access to the moorlands.

THE NATIONAL PARK WARDEN SERVICE

The first agreements to be made were with landowners in Edale, the Youth Hostels Association, who owned moorland behind Edale Youth Hostel, and the Duke of Devonshire. The National Parks and Access to the Countryside Act of 1949, which had established National Parks, also allowed for the appointment of wardens when access agreements were signed in order to ensure sound public behaviour and to assist the public in enjoying their moorland experience.

Burnley-born Tom Tomlinson, warden of Edale Youth Hostel, was appointed as the first full-time National Park warden in Britain. One of his first tasks was to convince his employers that a Land Rover was more appropriate to the job than a motorbike, on which he could not carry a stretcher. That accomplished, he set about enlisting support from local rambling clubs. On Good Friday 1954, ramblers gathered outside the Nag's Head Inn in Edale, along with politicians and National Park officials, to formally establish the first National Park warden service in the country, and Tom Tomlinson briefed the assembled ramblers.

Green and red 'National Park Warden' armbands were issued and the first patrols ventured up into the Grindsbrook Meadows to gaze at the southern slopes of Kinder, now open to the public for free access. Local hotel owner and campaigner for National Parks and access, Fred Heardman, had already established an unofficial information centre in what had once been the dining-room of the pub, and this became the first briefing centre for the embryonic warden service.

It was not long before teetotaller Tom moved his wardens across the road to Cooper's Café, where briefings took place on Saturday and Sunday mornings in

THE BOOK OF EDALE

Left: *Volunteers gather outside the Nag's Head Inn to witness the launch of the first National Park warden service in the country on Good Friday in 1954. The first head warden, Tom Tomlinson, is to the right of the young boy in a cap.*

Right: *National Park board members and officials at the warden service inauguration. Pictured are: Phil Daley (with armband), chair of the Access and Paths sub committee; John Foster, the National Park Director on his right; and Gerald Haythornthwaite of the Council for the Preservation of Rural England (far right).*

Left: *Fred Heardman, owner of the Nag's Head Inn and National Parks campaigner, points to the now-open moors as National Park head warden, Tom Tomlinson, looks on, 1954.*

Right: *Inauguration of the National Park warden service in 1954 outside the Nag's Head Inn.*

RECREATION

Tom Tomlinson, the National Park head warden, leads the first patrol of voluntary wardens on to the moors on Good Friday in 1954.

the steamy atmosphere of the two converted railway carriages that constituted the café. A giant kettle provided a welcome mug of tea after a cold, wet day spent patrolling the windy gritstone edges and misty labyrinth of peat groughs on the Kinder plateau.

During the first year more than 500 individual patrols were provided by 20 rambling organisations, but as the years progressed it became necessary to employ part-time paid staff to ensure adequate patrols. In 1958 Edale School provided the venue for training young aspiring wardens on the Cadet Warden Training Course, held over a number of weekends. The course consisted of instruction in 'the right manner' to approach visitors; methods of teaching people to appreciate the countryside; the art of hill walking, including map and compass use; the correct way in which a warden should use his or her powers and authority; and the fundamental principles of first aid and mountain rescue. Six patrols with experienced rangers were followed by an examination and the issue of a certificate.

Fieldhead became the focal point of the National Park's activities in Edale when it became the information and warden-briefing centre, and mountain-rescue post, all on one site and with a camp-site for visitors. On two afternoons a week the briefing centre also served as the local doctor's surgery.

Local government reorganisation brought changes to the National Park in 1974, and the warden service became the ranger service with a remit to cover not only the moorland access land but also the valleys and dales of the wider Peak National Park. At the time of writing the ranger service provides advice to visitors and support for farmers throughout the park, but Edale remains the spiritual home of the service and a walking Mecca for ramblers from all over the country.

FOOT-AND-MOUTH DISEASE

In 1967 Edale was devastated by the onslaught of foot-and-mouth disease and the valley was isolated to stop the disease from travelling unabated up the Pennines. Walking was banned and wardens manned the two entrances to the valley to explain the closure to visitors and to control entry. Disinfected straw was laid liberally across the road. The moors were once more closed for foot-and-mouth disease in 2001 but thankfully no cases were reported in the valley. During severe winters wardens also assisted in digging trapped sheep from snow and helping to get milk to the railway.

CUSTODIANS OF THE COUNTRYSIDE

An important aspect of the management of the moors and footpaths around Edale today is the undertaking of restoration work and conservation work by the Peak Park. Footpaths and bridle-ways with legal status are the responsibility of the Highways Authority, but the maintenance is undertaken by the National Park countryside maintenance team, rangers and volunteers. On the high moorland around Edale, and on Bleaklow, the National Trust and the National Park Pennine Way Maintenance Team have been undertaking specialised footpath and moorland restoration work since 1991, funded by the former Countryside Commission.

This concern for the Kinder, Bleaklow and Blackhill peat bogs and moorlands arose after the gradual realisation that the peat appeared to be eroding away in certain areas. Careful research proved that this was indeed happening. Numbers of walkers on the Pennine Way, roughly 10,000 doing the whole trail and 240,000 to 360,000 accessing popular sections each year, were wearing away the peat. Other areas were suffering from overgrazing, climate change, deep-seated fires and atmospheric pollution. Farmers entered into agreements to reduce the numbers of grazing sheep and temporarily fenced-off 'exclosures' were limed, fertilised and seeded with

Well-known walker and National Parks campaigner Fred Heardman in the old dining-room of the Nag's Head Inn which he had converted to an information centre prior to the development of the National Park Visitor Centre at Fieldhead.

Above: *Mr Pratt the cobbler talks to Fanny Clarke at the gate to Fieldhead House, now the National Park Visitor Centre.*

Right: *Fred Heardman and Sir John Hunt (later Lord Hunt) at the opening of Edale Barn, Upper Booth, 1961. It was used by Nottinghamshire schools for outdoor pursuits and by the Peak Wardens' Association.*

Below: *Stone flags in Grindsbrook Meadows.*

Below: *The log bridge, Grindsbrook.*

grass and heather by the Pennine Way team. This was done to slow down or stop the peat erosion and to encourage the heather to regenerate.

Walkers today encounter strange piles of stone slabs, bales of heather and huge white airlift bags of rock on steep slopes and high moorland. These are 'exclosures', created by the Upland Footpath Team from the Peak Park and teams from the National Trust to keep sheep out while the vegetation regenerates. The Moors for the Future Project is co-ordinating this restoration and conservation work on the moors around Edale and other areas of the Dark Peak. With the co-operation of walkers and visitors to the area, it is hoped that this unique and important landscape around Edale can be protected.

Mountain Rescue

For many years prior to the warden service, moorland rescues were carried out by local villagers. Many aircraft were to end their flights prematurely on the misty moors of the Peak District, and local villagers were often the first on the scene. In the mid-1960s wardens were involved in carrying off the two occupants of a Dragon Rapide aircraft, which was later destroyed by fire. In another case a small Cessna crashed in the hills above the village, and the two occupants walked relatively unscathed to the Nag's Head Inn for a brandy while unsuspecting firemen and police searched for the wreck. The wreck was salvaged by the local full-time wardens before it attracted public attention.

Many ill-equipped ramblers also went missing or sustained injuries and were carried to the village by farmers and other villagers. The tragic loss of three young lives on the Four Inns walk in 1964 culminated in a more formal mountain-rescue structure in the Peak District and the birth of Edale Mountain Rescue Team, consisting of National Park voluntary wardens, led by the deputy head warden, George Garlick. George had, from 1960, been living at Fieldhead, a site chosen as the first purpose-built National Park information centre, with a camp-site run by his wife Joyce.

The Edale Mountain Rescue Team, a voluntary group now independent of the National Park, responds to over 40 calls a year, many of those in Edale and the surrounding hills and moors. The team also provides safety stewards for the Edale Society's bi-annual beating the bounds around the high-level parish boundary.

Grouse Shooting

The heather-clad moors that rise above the Edale Valley are home to the only purely indigenous British bird, the red grouse. In the latter part of the nineteenth century, grouse shooting became fashionable and played an important part in the local economy, with gamekeepers being employed to construct and maintain shooting butts and burning the heather by rotation. Shooting cabins began to appear, often by springs and close to the lines of butts. One cabin, the highest in Derbyshire at 1,970 feet and situated in the meandering course of Grindsbrook before it descends to the valley, was built in around 1870 by Micah Tym of Edale. Although a deeply religious man he drank 'one above his nine' at 2p a pint in the Nag's Head one night. He woke with a great hangover but proceeded up the hill to work at the cabin. He was later joined by William Belfitt, the keeper, who poked fun at him only to receive a sermon on temperance. After this episode the cabin became known as Mike's Church. However, by 1930 the cabin was in a poor condition when Mr W.N.L. Champion employed four Edale men to repair it – Jack Burdikin, Jack Tym, Jack Wright Rowbottom and Jack Belfitt – and from then on it became known as Four Jacks Cabin, as it is referred to today. All that remains at the time of writing is the stone foundations. It is said that bottles of beer still lie buried close by from those early days.

Another significant cabin was built from wood and was situated in lower Grindsbrook at the foot of a clough known as Butt Clough and Millbrook – probably because of evidence of an old smelting place. Shooters would take sustenance in this cabin and photographs show serving maids at the door. One of the keepers, Bill Sims, actually lived in the cabin for a short time and coal was carried by horseback from the village to heat it. Another stone cabin was situated higher up the same clough, closer to the

Left: *Fieldhead House. The wooden annexe was used as a National Park voluntary wardens' briefing centre until its removal and replacement by the National Park Visitor Centre in 1966. Former head warden George Garlick, wife Joyce, and sons Roger and George junr lived in the house, followed by Ken Drabble and family. The mountain-rescue post was also moved to Fieldhead from its former home at the Nag's Head. The warden-briefing centre was used for many years as the local doctor's surgery for an hour every Tuesday and Friday until it moved to the village hall where it still takes place at the time of writing.*

Above: *Shooting lodge in Grindsbrook, early 1900s, now demolished. It was inhabited for a period by Bill Sims the gamekeeper.*

Left: *Arthur Lowe, gamekeeper, water bailiff and special constable in the early 1960s.*

Below: *Shooting party outside the Nag's Head in the early 1900s.*

RECREATION

Grouse-shooting party in Grindsbrook, c.1950s.

Right: *Frederick Sims, gamekeeper, with Nell in the early 1900s.*

Below: *Dr Laffety and gamekeeper Jack Belfitt in the upper reaches of Grindsbrook in the 1950s.*

Left: *Fred Heardman, known affectionately as 'Bill the Bogtrotter', stands at his bar in the Nag's Head Inn.*

Above: *Licence for Sarah Dain to sell ale at the Nag's Head in 1799.*

Left: *The Nag's Head in the 1930s.*

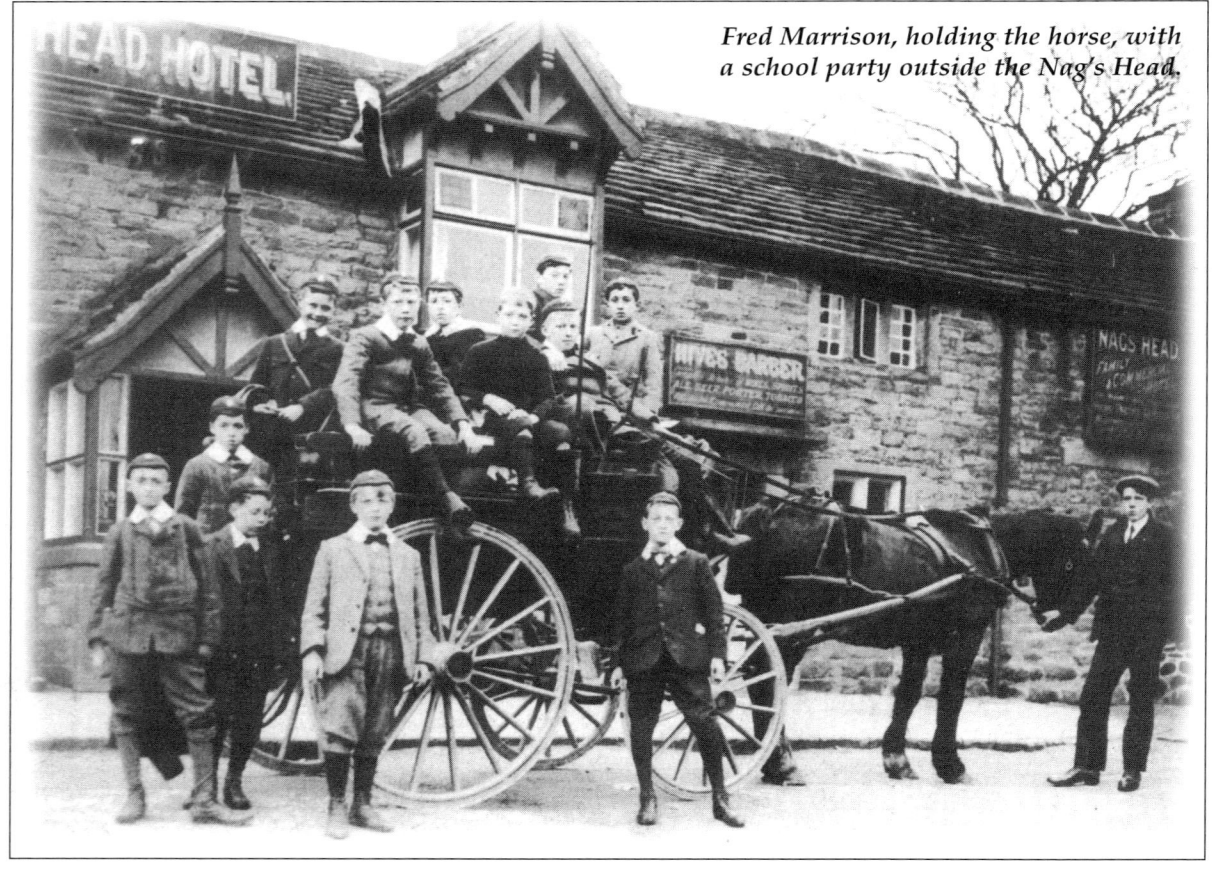

Fred Marrison, holding the horse, with a school party outside the Nag's Head.

RECREATION

Gamekeeper Jack Belfitt at Four Jacks Cabin on the Kinder plateau. He was one of the four 'Jacks' from Edale who rebuilt the cabin in 1930. Originally built by another Edale man, Micah Tym in 1870, this is the highest shooting cabin in Derbyshire.

now-defunct line of butts which were made from peat sods laid on top of each other to form a hide. The cabins were often situated near springs that rose from between the gritstone tors and the shale slopes – still a wonderful source of fresh drinking-water today.

Many of the cabins were used by hikers for temporary shelter and occasionally to sleep in, but sadly most were vandalised in the 1950s and time and the inclement weather brought about their final demise. Now the ruins provide markers for walkers on the often featureless plateau of Kinder Scout.

At the height of its popularity, grouse shooting provided employment for many local lads as beaters during the season running from 12 August to December – and providing an income that supplemented their meagre farm wages. For many it was the only time they ever went up on to the moors, while for others it was also a chance to check on their sheep.

Although grouse shooting has declined in the twenty-first century, the moors are still managed in a way that supports and encourages heather, thus ensuring that the grouse remain an important feature of any visit to the Kinder plateau. During the 1920s and '30s the mountain hare was reintroduced by grouse shooters after an absence of around 2,000 years. The hare, which turns white in winter, has found a niche in the rocky outcrops that fringe the plateau. Hares can often be seen grazing the moorland vegetation or sheltering from the wind in the peat groughs and boulders while the often very vocal male grouse survey their territories from prominent rises in the heather and bilberry.

Edale Inns

There are two licensed premises in Edale and have been for many years. The Old Nag's Head Inn, usually referred to as simply the Nag's Head, was probably originally a farmhouse in which ale was brewed to serve the packmen using the route from Cheshire into Yorkshire, which passed by the door. At one time a porch and bay windows were added to the pub. The eastern end of the building was once a smithy, and then became a storeroom. The wing pointing north was once stables and coach-house with a loft above, accessed by stone steps from the yard. Edale Band held practice sessions there.

In 1931 Fred Heardman became owner of the Nag's Head and the Church Hotel. The storeroom of the Nag's Head remained a store, but the stables were made into a sitting-room and the loft into four bedrooms. The stone steps disappeared. The coach-house remained as a garage, providing storage space for a truckload of coal and a large tank of paraffin to supply all the oil-lamps.

At one time there was a board over the door with the date 1660 but an earlier record was found carved into the lintel, which gave the date as 1577. However, there was almost certainly a building on the site before then.

During the war, a shortage of staff put an end to the catering and only the bar remained open, although at times the bedrooms were used as an overflow for the Church Hotel. Around 1950 Michael Jackson, an Edale resident and an art student, painted a horse's head over the porch and there has a been a sign with a horse's head at the pub ever since, although the breed of horse has varied.

In 1946 the Heardman family moved from the Church Hotel to the Nag's Head and after a time the dining-room became an unofficial information centre in conjunction with the Peak park until they took over Fieldhead. Until Fred's retirement in 1960 there was only a small bar and no beer pump at the Nag's Head. Beer was brought up by the glass from the cellar as needed, or in busy times in a gallon jug.

By 1960 more space was needed. Mr John Shentall bought the property, turned the storeroom into a large lounge and incorporated the small buildings at the back. There were a lot of alterations inside. The latest additions, by the owners at the time of writing, are two holiday cottages built at the back.

Members of a shooting party take a break at Four Jacks Cabin on Kinder shortly after it was rebuilt in 1930 by the four Edale 'Jacks'.

Edale Brass Band in the 1920s.

Edale Village Band in the 1920s/'30s.

RECREATION

A Village Footpaths meeting in the Nag's Head Inn in 1950. Left to right: ?, Mr Bentley, Fred Heardman, ?, Wilf Hulse.

Fred and Milly Heardman behind the bar at the Nag's Head Inn in the early 1950s.

Right: A Nag's Head Inn postcard with pre-war prices.

A ramblers' group with Fred Heardman outside the Nag's Head Inn in the mid-1950s.

101

At one time there was another inn in Edale known as the Church Inn, across the road from the old graveyard, where the original chapel once stood. At the time of writing this is a house called Church Cottage. At one time 'mine host' was expected to go to church before opening on a Sunday. With the coming of the railway a bigger place was needed and around 1893 a hotel was built near the station and the name, licence and the then landlady of the Church Inn, Mrs Joe Burdikin, moved into it. The Church Hotel was named after the Church Inn, and kept the name for many years.

Fred Heardman bought both the Church Hotel and the Nag's Head Inn in 1931, and so held two licences. The Church Hotel had its own generator, but this only supplied light – cooking was done on a large solid-fuel Aga. Across the yard was the annexe, consisting of one large room with three staff bedrooms over it. This room was furnished with trestle-tables and benches and was used at one time by large parties of ramblers who were staying at various guest-houses down the valley. A party of 80 came from Froggatt, until their guest-house there was burned down. Around 60 came from Moorgate in Hope, and another 40 from Birchfield. Neither of these is still a guest-house at the time of writing.

During the Second World War utility china was used at the Church Hotel. The utility cups had no handles and were shaped to stack easily – useful for carrying across the yard but notoriously unsuitable for drinking hot tea.

In 1945 the Church Hotel was sold to Mrs Brenda Harris, who later became Mrs Brenda Smith. She was the longest-serving owner/landlady in the history of the hotel and retired in 1972; she was renowned for her cooking.

After Brenda Smith retired the hotel changed hands a number of times and in turn became The Jolly Rambler, The Rambler Inn, and is called The Rambler Country House Hotel at the time of writing. The exterior of the building has changed little over the years, the main addition being a fire escape. The annexe is now staff accommodation; what was once a wash-house and another small outbuilding have been made into a holiday cottage. Inside, alterations have been more extensive.

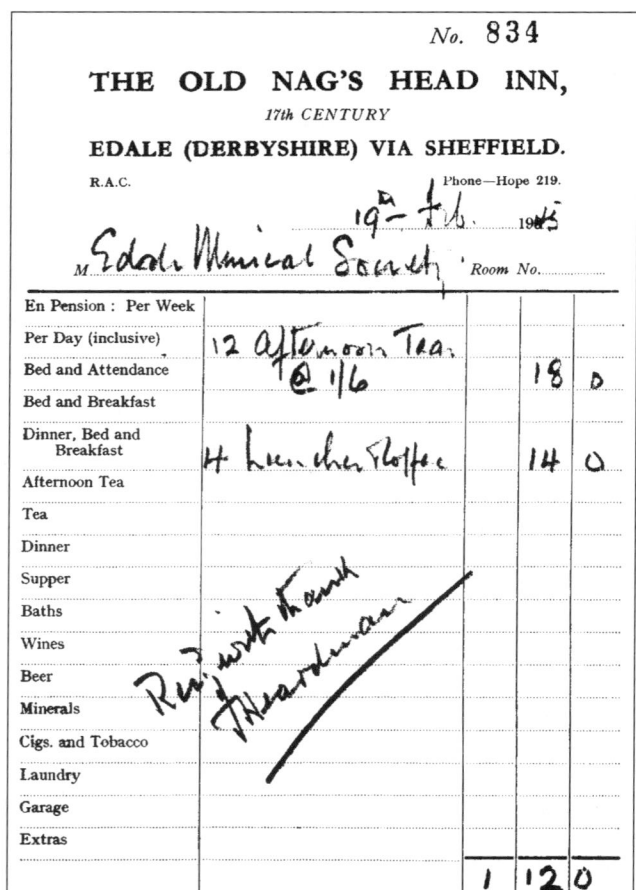

Above: *A bill from the Nag's Head Inn.*

Above: *Church Inn (Church Cottage at the time of writing) and the Burdikin family in 1896.*

Right: *Mrs Joe Burdikin in the late 1930s. She was the last licencee at the Church Inn (now Church Cottage) in around 1896, before she moved to the new Church Hotel, which was built shortly after the opening of the new railway.*

RECREATION

The Parish Church and Church Cottage (formerly the Church Inn).

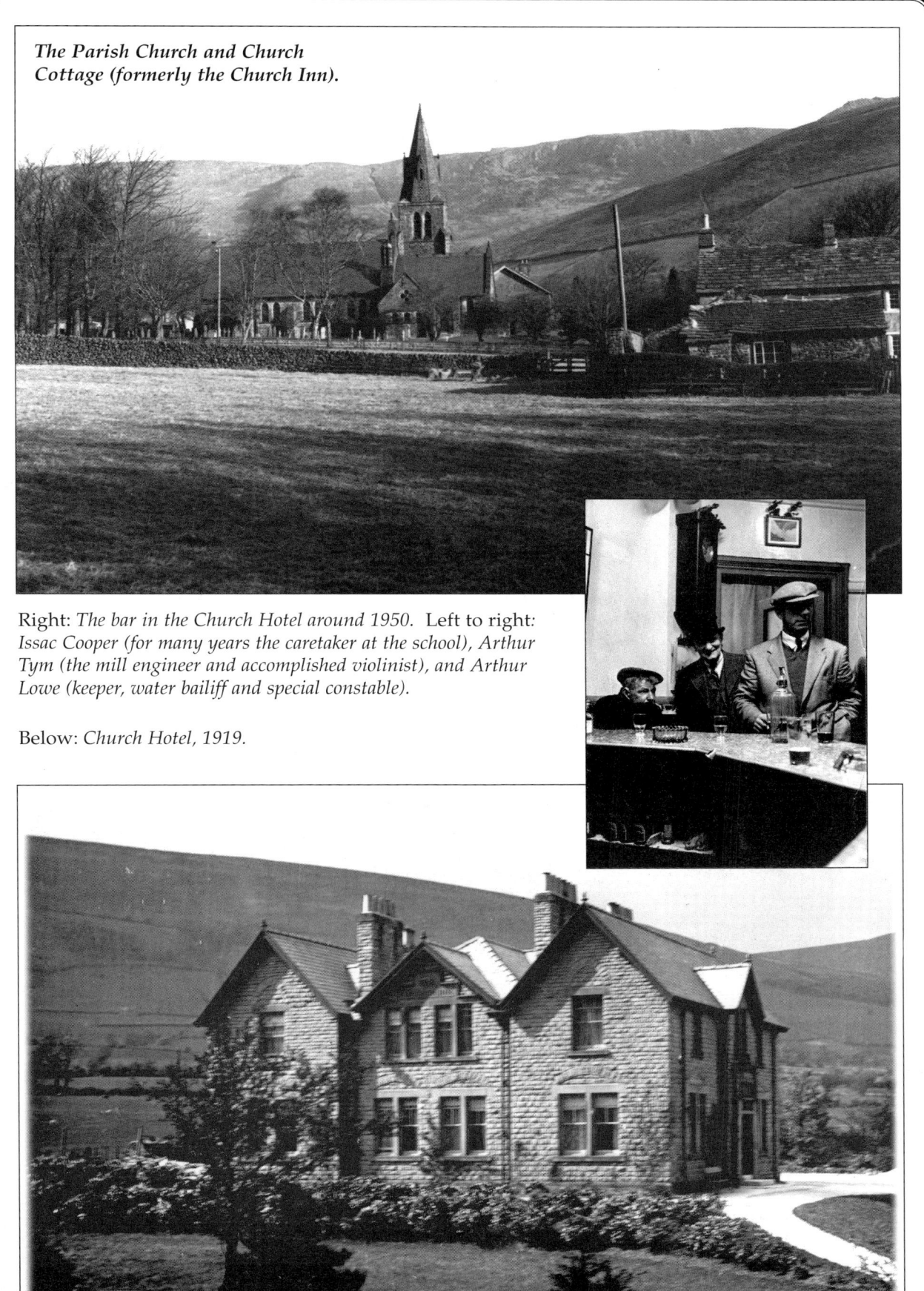

Right: *The bar in the Church Hotel around 1950. Left to right: Issac Cooper (for many years the caretaker at the school), Arthur Tym (the mill engineer and accomplished violinist), and Arthur Lowe (keeper, water bailiff and special constable).*

Below: *Church Hotel, 1919.*

103

Right: *British Legion dinner, 1956.*

Left: *British Legion dinner at the Church Hotel, 1956.*

Below: *Edale Barrel Race, 2001. Julian McIntosh receives the winner's trophy on behalf of his team as organisers Geoff Townsend* (back left) *and Clive Wetherall* (third from left, back) *look on.*

RECREATION

The Great Kinder Beer Barrel Challenge

A pub joke on a cold wet January night in 1999, when a disgruntled Geoff Townsend discovered the Nag's Head had run out of his favourite beer, was the beginning of the annual Great Kinder Beer Barrel Challenge. 'Well', said Geoff, 'I'll damn well run over to the Snake Pass Inn and bring a barrel back over the tops.' 'You do that, and I'll give you a free barrel of beer', retorted the landlord.

Never to be put down, Geoff planned and organised a race and got together a team of local friends. Using a stretcher to carry the full barrel, they ran from the Snake Pass to the Nag's Head in Edale, much to the astonishment of the landlord and many others! As well as getting 72 free pints to drink, the team raised £1,200 for Edale Primary School. Having proved it could be done, Geoff threw down the gauntlet to anyone who could raise a team and reckoned they could run the course. So the challenge was born in 2000 with seven teams, each eight strong, competing.

It is not as easy as it sounds. The challenge starts with an exhausting 750-foot climb to a height of 1,850 feet. It then involves pounding over a punishing terrain of peat bogs and rough, rocky ground before a steep descent to the Nag's Head at 950 feet carrying a barrel weighing 100lbs. Although only five miles in distance, it is a gruelling test of stamina, strength and fitness. The teams even have to make their own carrier to hold the 100lb barrel.

Insurance cover being possible, it is hoped to throw open the challenge to all of the villages in the Hope Valley. This is a unique race, over some of the most beautiful but toughest hill country in Britain. And the teams insist that it is fun!

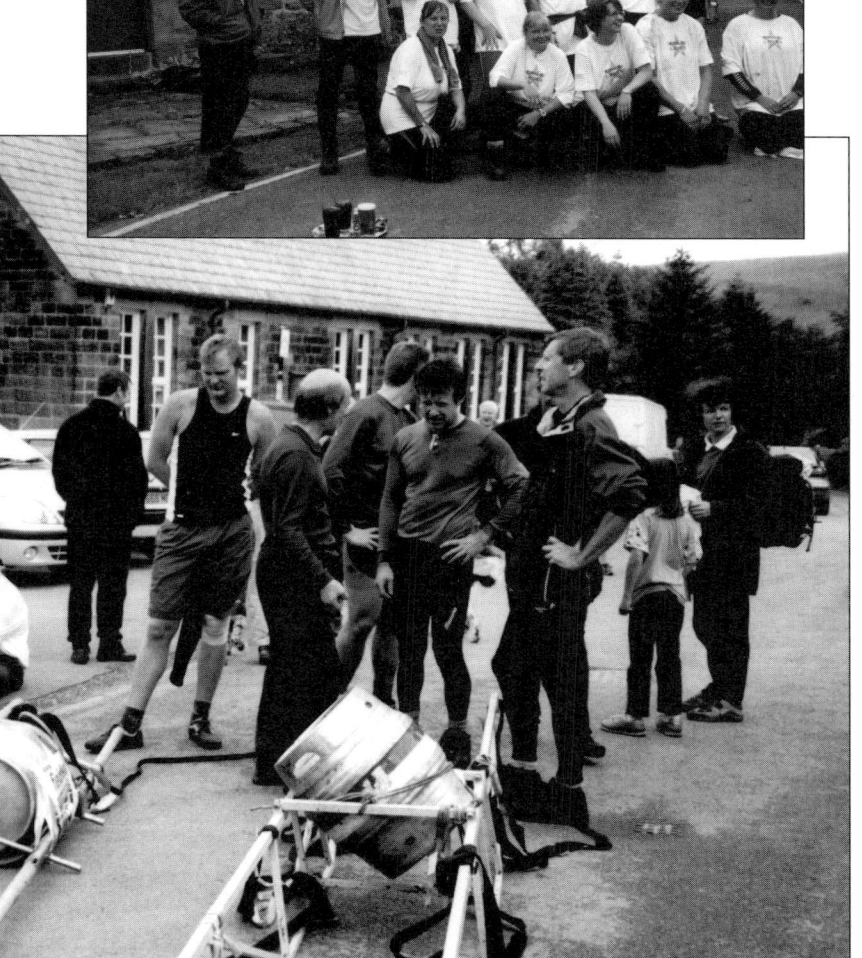

Right: *Edale Barrel Race, 2001. The Edale ladies' team and supporters pose for the cameras at the end of a well-run race.*

Below: *Edale Barrel Race, 2001. Villagers Julian McIntosh, Dave Crossland and Richard Grimes take a well-earned rest by their barrel after completing the race.*

Edale Music Hall in the late 1980s. Dr Horace Jackson (holding the papers) closes the performance.

Left: *Amy Tym and Mary Bentley in front of the Reading Room.*

Below: *Music hall social evening in the 1980s.*

Chapter Eight

CLUBS AND SOCIETIES

No television? No trains? And several miles to the next village. What on earth did the people of Edale do for entertainment in the days before transport and technology provided easy links with the outside world? As in all isolated communities, they became adept at entertaining themselves.

During the last century village amusements included a musical society, a drama club, and a Women's Institute. The last two are still going at the time of writing and there is also a tennis club and the Edale Society. The Edale Horticultural Society is one of the oldest in the country, and the Edale Pantomime production possibly the most notorious.

THE READING ROOM

Edale Public Library and Reading Room was once the hub of the village social life. But there was a problem – the Reading Room was for men only. Built in around 1863 by the Champion family on their own land at the rear of the Nag's Head Inn, the wooden building included a billiard table and a library and was for the use of young men and as a boys' club. In the late-nineteenth century Parish Council meetings, naturally all male, were also held there.

All was tranquil until something happened that put Edale in the national news. The women rebelled. The following is a quote from the *Sunday Chronicle*:

Invaders turned out – and kept out for 40 years
Sunday Chronicle *Special Correspondent,*
Edale – Saturday

'We're having no women in here' said the dart thrower. 'That's right, no petticoat government in here' said the billiards player.
And to a chorus of 'Ayes' the monarchs of Edale (Derbyshire) took their stand against a threatened feminine onslaught on their masculine stronghold.

However the *Daily Express* told a different story:

Where woman dare not enter – but she did.
Edale equality fight... Men lose first round in meeting place battle.
Once again has the peace of the village of Edale, in the Derbyshire hills, been destroyed. For 70 years the men of the village have found sanctuary when needed, at the end of a day's work, in the village reading room – the one place in the village where the shadow of a woman dare not fall.

Throughout the long years this law has been inviolate. But time is no respecter of persons and with the passing years the number of men using the place has gradually decreased. Only the old and infirm resort to its seclusion today. In this 'perm' and petrol age, the young men of the village have no use for tradition, and the old men tire of their own company, decided to close the room.

The annual meeting was in progress when, to the consternation of all, two women entered. Never before had such a thing occurred. The members of the committee, the treasurer and the secretary – who had held their positions for 25 years – resigned immediately. The meeting had just re-elected its president for the year and it was he who bore the brunt of the first attack of the women of Edale in their fight for equality. They are determined, they intimated, to be as other women in this modern age. They have their Women's Institute, their drama group and their Rural Communities Council. They need a meeting place and intend to have it. The old men of the village withered before the attack. Age was useless against youth. They beat a hasty retreat and women having now tasted the first fruits of victory, are seeking to consolidate their position in this secluded vale.

And that is the story of how Edale Reading Room was opened up to women. Later in the 1930s whist drives were a regular feature in the Reading Room. Children visited at Christmas for teas before going to the school where there was dancing and games – followed by a scramble for sweets and a final dance, called 'Sir Roger de Coverley'.

The Reading Room finally came into disuse. Many large events such as the flower show, whist drives and dances continued to be held in the school and a large wooden hall built on to the original Cooper's Café became the venue for other events prior to the building of a village hall. The wooden Reading Room was finally demolished in the early 1970s.

THE EDALE MUSICAL SOCIETY

The first meeting of the Edale Musical Society took place on 1 October 1943. The meeting was held at

107

Reading Room Accounts & Receipts

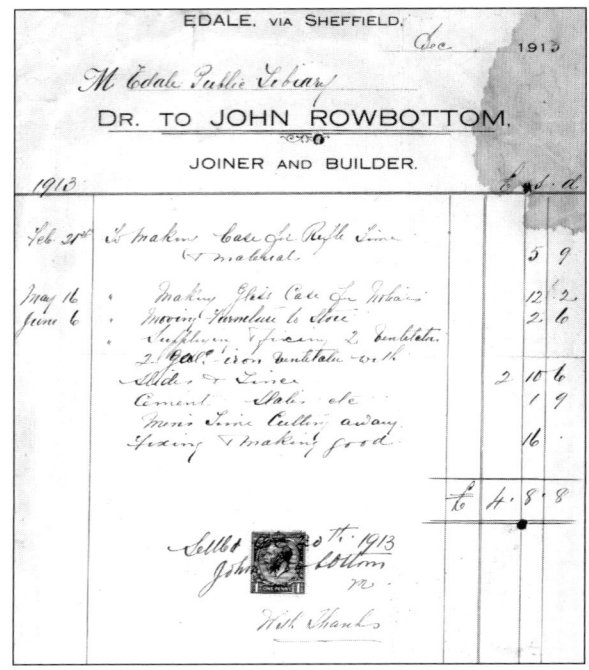

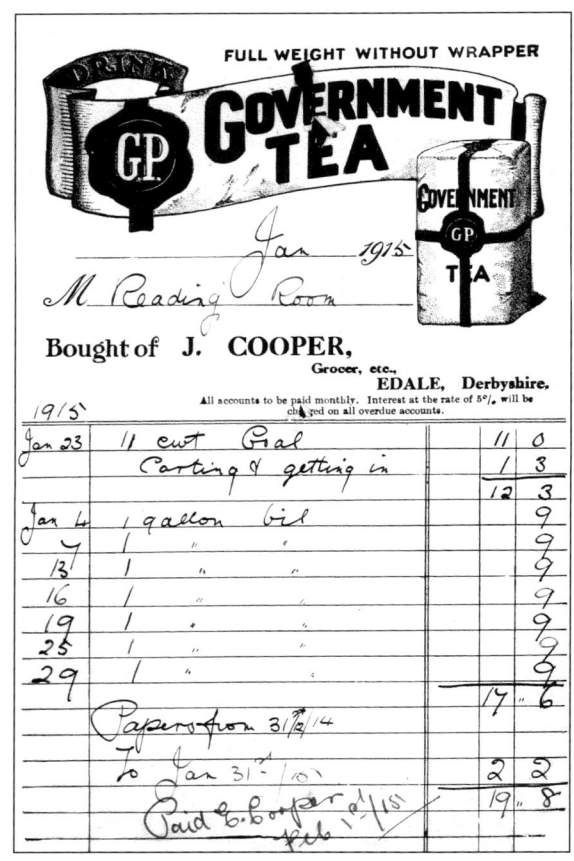

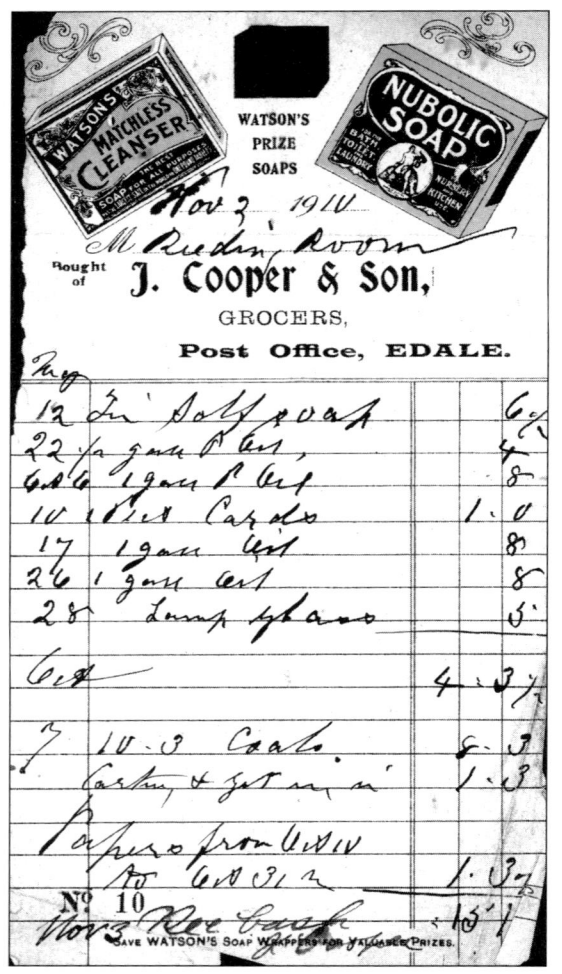

CLUBS AND SOCIETIES

Edale music hall Names in the village hall in the late 1980s. Left to right: *David Mount, Jo Falzon, Revd Adrian Murray-Leslie, Denise Bee, Rob Jackson, Glynis Ballantyne.*

'Endcliff', the home of Captain Walker. The captain was responding to a desire expressed by the residents of Edale for the revival of the 'practice and performance of music' in the village. A subscription of two shillings and sixpence (12$^{1}/_{2}$p) to be paid per season – from 1 October to 30 April – was agreed.

The 12 people present at the representative gathering were as follows: Mrs Walker, Mr and Mrs Dobbs, Mrs Greenstreet, Miss Shirt, Mrs Day, Mrs W. Sims, Mrs J. Prior, Mrs A. Tym, Miss J. Rowbottom, Mr Harvey and Captain Walker.

By the end of the meeting Captain Walker had been elected president; Mrs J. Prior, treasurer; Mrs Ness-Walker, secretary; Mr Elcock, conductor; and Mrs Elcock, 'accompanist'. As a piano teacher in her own right, Mrs Elcock gave lessons to many of the local children. Geoff Sims, son of Mrs W. Sims, was one of those children taught by her.

Mrs Walker proposed a resolution, which was read out by Captain Walker, the president:

... that The Edale Musical Society be free of any special denomination, that it may produce music in any church, chapel or Christian building and that it be run in a free atmosphere of co-operation as good as the music it hopes to produce.

The president went on to say that the society was formed to produce 'classical music' and to avoid what he termed as 'jazz' and 'dance music', or 'any type of music of that description'. He also explained that 'the society would not be governed by any form of church but would be a village musical society.'

A member agreed, pointing out that there was plenty of dance music and jazz in the village school at dances, for those who were fond of that sort of thing – it was generally agreed that 'that type of music' be cut out from the programme of the Edale Musical Society.

At the fourth meeting of the society on 24 November 1943, a performance of Handel's 'Messiah' was discussed, and it was decided to perform some part of that work in the church on Sunday, 16 January 1944. We can only guess as to how the performance went, because at the next meeting, on 20 January, Handel's 'Messiah' was not mentioned. However, the state of the church organ was discussed at length. Despite being seen by an 'expert' prior to the rehearsal on the Saturday, the organ was still giving trouble and it had been necessary to 'telephone Sheffield' that same afternoon. The vicar reported that a man had been out on the Sunday as a result of several telephone calls but did not say what the man had done to the organ.

A proposal by the vicar that a letter of appreciation should be sent to Mrs Jackson, the organist, 'for very hard work under difficult circumstances' was agreed.

In January 1944 Revd A.W. Kilby requested that in future he should be referred to as 'The Vicar' and not by name. No reason was given.

Meetings must have been a lively affair, as during the same meeting the president had to appeal to the committee to not all talk at once. He added that he had 'already brought up this matter on two previous occasions' and he 'hoped it would not have to be brought up again.'

Another cause for concern within the society was whether or not to hold further performances in the church. The vicar proposed that future performances such as 'The Creation', 'Crucifixion' or 'The Elijah' be considered. The president had to point out that more performances in the church might be 'misconstrued' by those society members who did not belong to the Church of England. However, due to a lack of another suitable venue, the church it had to be.

During the war years the Edale Musical Society played its part, and a receipt from G. Shirt, of Crowden Lea, tells us that the society donated £2.2s.0d. to the 'Welcome Home Fund'.

Minutes of a meeting on 1 May 1945 tell us that an ENSA concert for the troops had been held in the schoolroom, not the church. This raised £7.10s.0d. which was equally divided between the Red Cross and the Edale Comfort Fund, which had been founded to send parcels to Edale soldiers and was run by John (Jack) Tym.

When the society met on 16 September 1946, they voted to continue for the 1946/47 season and to hold the AGM in the schoolroom. Mr Harris of the Church Hotel was approached regarding rehearsals being held in the café (a wooden building next to the hotel), providing it could be heated.

There are no more records of any meetings held after 27 April 1948, when Mrs W. Sims, the secretary, recorded that the attendance was 'good'. A programme of light opera was discussed and a further meeting planned for 1 June 1948.

Another document exists relating to an earlier musical society in Edale. This is dated 1933 and refers to the society's bank book with the first entry dated 13 January 1933.

Above: *Edale Women's Institute, 1943. Left to right, back row: Mrs Shirt, Gert Rowbottom, Mrs Berghaus, Sarah Gee, Muriel Shirt, Madge Elliott; middle row: Gladys Cooper, ?, Agnes Rowbottom, Rhoda Broome; front row: Mrs Harvey, Joan Bucknell, Sarah Sims, Jean Frankish with baby, Norman Cooper (lying down).*

Below: *Edale Women's Institute, founded in 1933, celebrating their diamond jubilee in 1993. Left to right, back row: Milly Heardman, Belinda Critchlow, Eileen Hodgson, Barbara Neves, Phylis Howe, Norah Earl, Glynis Ballantyne; front row: Caroline Jackson, Angela Inskip, Pat Atkin, Jean Chapman, Ella Inskip, Eileen Hickenson, Dorothy Baird, Joan Williams, Maureen Young, Martha Tym (the oldest member, at 99, cutting the cake – Martha lived until she was 101), Amy Tym, Winnie Cotterill, Judith Shirt, Val Gilbert, visitor, Ivy Kincaid.*

EDALE WOMEN'S INSTITUTE

Edale Women's Institute was formed in 1933 and celebrated its 70th birthday in 2003. There was already a WI at Hope, which had been going for ten years, and there were WIs at Bamford and Chinley. In the days before television, little transport and no night classes, it provided an opportunity for the women of the village to get together, meet different people, and learn much from interesting speakers and courses.

The main founder member was probably Helen Heardman, the mother of the president at the time of writing. Edale WI has continued to meet, despite a fluctuating membership. In the past there have been as many as 40 members. Efforts have been made to increase membership, including moving the meetings from afternoons to the evenings.

Edale WI enjoys excellent speakers and varied outings. It has participated in both county and national events, and has supported many national campaigns, among them one to keep local Post Offices open, and for pensioners to be able to collect pensions and benefits in cash.

The slogan on the WI county newsletter is 'Enlightenment, Friendship and Fun', and members feel that this sums it all up. Another favoured slogan is 'Today's women working for tomorrow's world'.

Meetings have been held in a number of places, starting in the original Cooper's Café and then the front room of the Church Hotel. The WI moved to the village hall after its opening in 1967.

THE EDALE SOCIETY

The Edale Society, founded in 1975, has provided a forum for Edale inhabitants to collect and share their knowledge of the parish. The society meets regularly to study various aspects of the valley, from the social and natural history, the industrial past, and local history in general. Major exhibitions to mark the church and railway centenaries have been researched and displayed by the society. Notable speakers are invited to come and talk about various issues related to the sections of the society.

The Edale Society continues to collect old archives of the valley and to add to the written and oral records, both past and present. This collection has created a unique portrait of the area and is becoming increasingly detailed. At the time of writing a recorded study of walls, hedges and field names is being made, while members of the natural history group have recorded most of the flowers in the valley, although new discoveries are made regularly. A popular field trip is made every year to a local farm, which has a particularly rich botanical history.

In those years when there is no boundary walk the Edale Society holds a Victorian/Edwardian picnic. Everyone has an opportunity to dress up in period costume and take a traditional picnic to a secluded and picturesque part of the valley. Children play Victorian and Edwardian games while the adults relax.

The first meeting of the calendar year is hosted by Edale Youth Hostel at Rowland Cote, when an

CLUBS AND SOCIETIES

Above: *Edale Society Victorian/Edwardian Picnic, c.1990.* Left to right, back row: *Luke Archer, Matthew Rumble, Beth Hardy, Hannah Rumble, Emma Hardy, Erica Rumble, Naomi Miller;* front row: *Bella Hardy, Elizabeth Archer*

Above: *Edale Society Victorian/Edwardian Picnic in Crowden Brook (Upper Booth Farm) in 1992.*

Right: *Edale Society Victorian/Edwardian Picnic at Dale Head Farm, 1992.*

Left: *Shelagh Gregory, Ashlyn Bower, Milly Heardman and Linda Read take a break with part-time ranger Robert Johnson at a checkpoint during the Edale Society's beating of the bounds.*

Left: *Edale Society beating the bounds in 1997. Pictured are the oldest entrant, Milly Heardman (aged 83), with the youngest, Oliver Mount (aged 5), near the end of the arduous 16-mile walk on Mam Tor summit. The walk is held every two years in June or September.*

Above: *Participants prepare to start the first 16-mile Edale Society beating the bounds walk around the high-level parish boundary in 1989. Local farmer Alan Atkin kindly allows the society to use his land in the only part of the walk which is not open to the public.*

Top: *Edale Society beating the bounds. Lunchtime on the first walk in 1989.*

Above: *Pauline Jackson and Amy Tym on the walk in 1989.*

excellent meal is followed by a guest speaker. This is an opportunity for members to socialise and to keep up with developments at the hostel, one of the most popular in the country. Rowland Cote provided hospitality in bygone days when the house belonged to the Batchelor family, of tinned food fame. Local resident, Val Gilbert, has a childhood memory of the Batchelor family sending the Rolls Royce down the drive to pick up local youngsters so that they could play with the children in the big house.

Beating the Bounds

Every two years a group of 60–70 locals walk the hilltops around the parish boundary. This popular event, known as the beating the bounds, was started in 1989 by the Edale Society. The 16-mile circular walk starts close to the Iron-Age hill-fort of Mam Tor and traverses the ridge that encloses the south side of the Vale of Edale. It then crosses the forbidding but unique peatlands of Kinder Scout, passing the highest point in Derbyshire at 2,088 feet above sea level.

Edale Mountain Rescue Team provides checkpoints across the featureless plateau. A steep descent to the River Noe at Edale End, the lowest part of the walk, is followed by an equally steep climb back to high ground. A local farmer kindly permits the walk to pass over his land on the only section that does not have public access. Beating the bounds provides a challenge to both young and old, with everyone following the same route. The youngest walker in 2003 was five, the oldest 83. For many, this walk is the only time they get to see the remote and spectacular boundary of their parish.

Edale Horticultural Society

Edale boasts the oldest village horticultural society in the country and has held annual produce shows for 146 years. The first show day was on the last Saturday in August, 1857. Ever since, the last Saturday in August has been a red-letter day in the Edale calendar.

While other village societies have closed through lack of support and finance, the Edale Horticultural Society show day continues to prosper and to bring together all the people of Edale, in friendly competition. This is no mean feat in a small village in a valley 800 feet above sea level, with short summers and frosts persisting until early June and usually returning in September. Coupled with heavy rainfall and strong Pennine winds, the show is a tribute to the skills and persistence of Edale gardeners and cooks. The broad

CLUBS AND SOCIETIES

The Horticultural Society centenary at Edale School in 1957 with morris dancers entertaining the visitors.

Left: *Edale Horticultural Society centenary flower show in the school, 1957.*

EDALE HORTICULTURAL SOCIETY

100th ANNUAL SHOW

Saturday, August 31st, 1957

at 2.30 p.m.

Admission 2/-   Children 6d.

Edale Horticultural Society's 1857–1957 centenary schedule.

Left: *Edale Horticultural Society centenary, 1957. Left to right: Anne Bowers, Lew Tyas, Amy Tym, Gwen Cooper, Jim Quarmby.*

113

variety of classes gives the show a wide appeal. There is something for everyone, from vegetable and flower arrangements to domestic categories and wine making. The children's section includes not only growing and cooking, but also crafts and creative skills.

The early shows had a limited range of vegetables and flowers, plus – amazingly for Edale – apples, pears and plums, but no domestic classes. Eggs, butter and bread classes were introduced in 1911, and the jam class was started in 1946. It was not until 1947 that a full domestic range was introduced and a specific children's section was brought in for the centenary show in 1957.

Prizes in the early days were all individually donated. Although mainly money, they also included tea sets, cutlery, steel shovels, scissors, 1lb tins of tea and even a dress length in material.

Highlights in the society's history were the centenary show in 1957, held in the school and Cooper's Café, and a live broadcast from Edale of the BBC's long-running, highly popular 'Gardeners' Question Time'. The centenary was celebrated in style with morris dancers, Edale Band playing during the show, and special rose and dahlia displays from Proctors and from Schofield, local garden centres. A resounding success, the 100th show day concluded with a dinner and dance to the music of the Ace Dance Band. It was a truly memorable marking of a major event in the life of Edale's long-treasured societies.

Treasurer Clive Wetherall says that the society is looking forward to the 150th show in 2007 and hopefully the return of the BBC. The society's activities have been significantly broadened since the late 1980s. The introduction of the seedling sale (bought in largely from a commercial nursery), on which many Edale people depend for their vegetable and flower plants, was a success from its outset. The proceeds from this are essential for the funding of prize monies at the annual show.

There is an annual trip to botanical gardens and a free 'Gardeners' Evening' with a guest speaker. Although it is vital for the future of the society that it stays financially solvent, the members' view is that, wherever possible, excess profits should be returned to the village in the form of free and subsidised activities and worthwhile prize monies. Even in 1884, some of the show-day profits were donated to the Church Building Fund.

Prize monies paid out on show day average from £180–£200, a generous amount compared with other societies' prizes. Show-day entries average around 240 exhibits and the exhibitors span all ages and interests. The show day is the one village activity that appeals to everyone, either as exhibitors or admirers, and with such strong support there is every indication that the society will continue to prosper and flourish and that parishioners will continue to benefit from the oldest of Edale traditions.

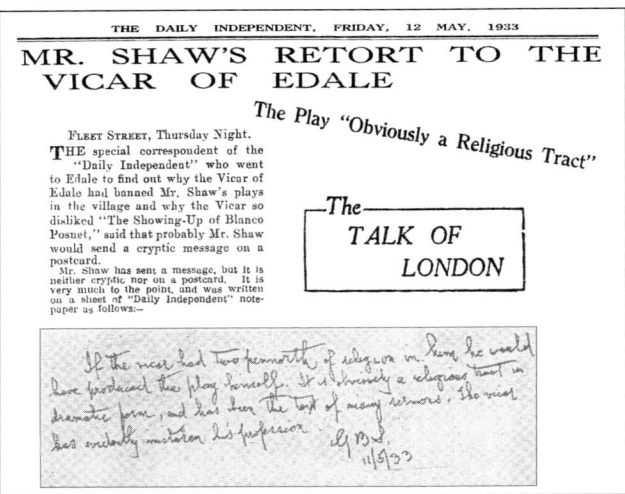

Cuttings taken from the Daily Independent *on Friday 12 May 1933, with George Bernard Shaw's response to the vicar of Edale.*

THE EDALE VILLAGE DRAMATIC GROUP

At first, all went well. The secretary of the newly-formed society acquired a loose-leaf notebook and labelled it 'Minute Book of the Edale Village Dramatic Group, September 7th 1932.' Printed on the inside cover, the manufacturer gives a reference number for ordering extra pages at 6d. for 100 sheets; this was useful information, as things turned out.

Three months later the society put on its first production. This consisted of three short dialect plays, *Honest Folk*, *A Village Jumble* and *Where There's A Will There's A Way*, which were performed in the school. These seem to have been well received and a local paper report of the time noted that:

... the consistently high quality of the performance spoke well for the ability and perseverance of the Group, and particular credit is due to Mrs Heardman, the organiser and producer... Mr. Harvey added to the pleasure of the entertainment by giving selections on the violin, accompanied by Miss Earnshaw on the piano, and Mrs P. Broom contributed pianoforte solos.

This seemed a promising start. Heartened, the players decided to choose a more challenging work for their second production, and later in 1933 the Edale Village Dramatic Group presented *The Showing Up of Blanco Posnet* by George Bernard Shaw in the village school. From here, the story is best told by extracts from the national press:

George Bernard Shaw Play Angers Vicar
Edale, Derbyshire

... The trouble began when Bernard Shaw's play 'The Showing Up of Blanco Posnet' was performed in the village school room... Dissentients told the vicar, who declared it to be blasphemous... GBS was brought into the

CLUBS AND SOCIETIES

Left: *Kinder Players' production of* The Duke's Dilemma *in 1934. Left to right, back row: Vic Noblett, Winifred Critchlow, George Hawtin, Harold Allsop, James Prior, Wright Dearnley, Maggie Prior, Arthur Rowbottom, Phyllis Rowbottom, Revd C. Frith, Mrs James Carrington, Martha Tym, Gladys Cooper, Stationmaster W. Chambers, Mrs Lem Tym with Mrs R.J. Cooper behind, James Carrington junr, Mrs Fred Rowbottom; front row: Ivy Rowbottom, Margaret Sims, Ruth Tym, Jean Rowbottom, Margaret Harvey, Mrs William Sims.*

Left: *Kinder Players at Hope Carnival in 1956.*

Below: *Kinder Players' social evening in Cooper's Café in the early 1930s.*

Kinder Players, 1956.

Left: *Kinder Players in the 1954 production of* Who Is Going To Pay.

Below: *Kinder Players perform the* The Camel's Back *in 1946*.

'war' and letters from Mrs F. Heardman (the president of the Edale Drama Group) reached him in the remotest parts of the world... His usual post card read, 'The whole matter is absurd'...
(*Daily Express*, 12 October 1933)

After the production of Shaw's play, the vicar and school managers decided to take action:

Vicar Wants to Censor Shows
Edale's amateur dramatic enthusiasts are wondering where they are going to perform their plays and hold their meetings this winter... The Vicar, the Rev. C. A. Frith is... instituting a system of censorship over all the plays, lectures, talks and readings which are to be held in the church (school).
(*Daily Independent*, 13 October 1933)

Drama Group Will Not Be Censored
... the drama group object to the censorship, and are determined to fight it. Plans are likely to be made for holding 'censored' plays in a big garage, so that there can be no interference. 'It is quite unfair to us,' said Mrs Heardman. 'The vicar has decided to become the Lord Chamberlain of the Peak, blue-pencilling and sub-editing the work of distinguished authors. But if we cannot use the schoolroom, we will look elsewhere. Edale will otherwise have to be content with 'sweet country drama', while other villages are becoming modern'.
(*Daily Express*, 12 October 1933).

Eventually, things settled down and the Edale Village Drama Group (soon to rename themselves the 'Kinder Players') went on to delight and entertain the village for many years.

The last entry, made in the same loose-leaf notebook that was used at the inaugural meeting, was in 1958. The saddest entry records the death of founder member and first president, Helen Heardman (Mrs F. Heardman):

Committee Meeting 11 October 1949
This meeting has been called to decide whether or not to carry on with the play owing to the tragic death of Mrs

Kinder Players in the 1957 production of Bonaventure.

Kinder Players' programme for Tomb with a View.

Heardman as the result of a motoring accident. It was decided that it would be Mrs Heardman's wish that the show must go on... Five members of the committee represented the Kinder Players at the cremation of Mrs Heardman at Stockport.

THE KINDER PLAYERS IN THE TWENTY-FIRST CENTURY

The Kinder Players were resurrected in 1991, after a lapse of several years. The revival was due partly to the arrival in the village of Judy and Phil Oldroyd from Yorkshire, where Judy had studied and taught drama in the West Riding. The other reason for the re-launch of the group was the enormous enthusiasm and range of dramatic talents in the village at the time.

One or two members of the new group, including Milly Heardman and Amy Tym, remember the original Kinder Players, when Helen Heardman and the other pioneers had so upset the vicar and school managers some 50 years before. At the time of writing things are very different for the society, in which the vicar, Adrian Murray-Leslie, and headmistress of Edale School, Sandra Pillans, are leading performers.

The plays chosen for the launch performance were *From Here to the Library* and *This Desirable Cottage*, directed by Judy, with scenery by designer Adrian Smith. The choice proved popular and was followed by various productions, including Dennis Potter's *Blue Remembered Hills*, also directed by Judy; Noel

Above: *Kinder Players' performance of* Blue Remembered Hills *in March 1997.* Left to right: *Lyn Widdowson, Phil Oldroyd, Glynis Ballantyne, Joe Hardy, Ashlyn Bower, David Mount.*

Left: *Poster for* Blue Remembered Hills, *1997.*

Coward's *Blythe Spirit*, directed by Glynis Ballantyne and Tricia Murray-Leslie; and Harold Pinter's *A Slight Ache*, directed by John Payne.

A century after the arrival of the railway in Edale, the event was celebrated with a performance of *Off The Rails*, a revue written by local author, Simon Jackson. The Kinder Players also organise regular prose and poetry evenings during which the audience sit at candlelit tables and enjoy supper and a glass of wine.

Edale Pantomime

It was never 'pantomime' except in the metaphorical sense – a group of people doing very silly things in public – and it began with the football club of 1974 staging an all-male Edale version of 'Snow White and the Eleven Dwarfs'. No one is quite sure why it wasn't strangled at birth; an early attempt to have it banned on the grounds of cruelty to the audience was foiled when a representative of the Lord Chamberlain's office asked 'Which one of you is David Chapman?' and eleven burly footballers all stepped forward together. No one has ever taken the blame for starting it but many, many Edalians, young and old, have played their part in perpetuating this no-holds-barred review of village life.

Early shows were written in rhyming couplets, song music shamelessly stolen from Sir Arthur Sullivan and tunelessly reproduced with words marginally more appropriate to the plot by various anonymous hacks with no apologies to W.S. Gilbert. Later, songs were borrowed from almost everywhere, plagiarised, half digested and regurgitated without credit or royalty being paid – the only reason the pantomime group has never been sued for infringement of copyright seems to have been that either the copy or the performance was so bad that no one could recognise the original any more!

The finale of the pantomime Treasure Island, *1988/9.*

Pantomime Treasure Island *with Revd Adrian Murray-Leslie as 'the missionary in the pot', 1988/9.*

CLUBS AND SOCIETIES

John Noakes (whose namesake was an early vicar in Edale) with Shep and National Park Ranger Gordon Miller during filming for a television episode of 'Go with Noakes' on the Pennine Way in 1976.

The opportunities for humour within such a format are almost limitless. The Edale show has milked parody of local personalities – frequently persuading them to portray themselves on the stage. The vicar appeared as missionary soup in a cannibals' cooking pot on 'Treasure Island' (don't even try to remember natives in the original), the National Park chief ranger as 'Gordon the Warden', lost – 'Who is this fellow so uncouth? Is this the way to Barber Booth?', and the oldest inhabitant of the valley – 'Name?', 'Milly Heardman', 'Age?', '247'.

The vehicles over the years for picking fun, satirising and generally behaving foolishly have been 'Snow White', 'Robin Hood', 'Kinderella', 'Treasure Island', 'Robin Hood' again, 'Aladdin', 'Treasure Island' again, 'Sinbad the Sailor', 'Robin Hood and the Arrows of Time' (millennium production), 'Edale Family Robinson', 'The Alternative Wizard of Oz' and possibly more or even less – no one is really quite sure any more.

And it has changed over the years; animals, women and younger people were slowly admitted to the cast in that order, and the total numbers of people participating in one way or another have fluctuated between 40 and 80, give or take a few. The budget for the 1974 production was £70 – 26 years later, the millennium production cost just over £700, but this is academic; the one thing we can guarantee is standing room only on all three nights.

Productions have not been without controversy; the shows have of course been irreverent and rude, but also challenging, picking fun at pomposity and stretching the boundaries of village taste. In a relatively isolated community the size of Edale, nothing much happens that isn't round the parish in 24 hours.

The pantomime offers an opportunity to put the mutterings on to the stage, exposing gossip and daring to comment publicly on the personal foibles we were all commenting on privately anyway. Nothing has really been barred – although there was an incident one year when the script-writing team was prevailed upon to cut comments about the purchase of a couple of horses. Hang on, this is an agricultural community – what could possibly be so threatening about buying horses? Well, nothing, only the husband knew nothing about it.

There was a concerted effort to abort the 1976 production of 'Robin Hood' in rehearsal. Responding to pre-production hype which hinted at indecent content, 'responsible' elements in the community tried to stop the show by withholding the fuses for the lighting board – the board belonged to the youth club and the pantomime team didn't have permission. Excuses prevailed – it was unsafe; the floor of the hall was being damaged by the scenery makers; etc, etc. But satire is the obvious weapon of choice against pomposity – and within hours the incident was written into the script, substitute fuses were found from somewhere, a tame electrician gave the lighting grid a clean bill of health, the youth club agreed to use of lights and the show, of course, went on.

The modern show is still uniquely Edale and written by local authors including Mark Wallington and Simon Jackson – if you live further away than Bradwell the chances are you won't get a single joke. Everyone who wants a part can be pretty well guaranteed an appearance but there's always the risk you will end up the butt of the joke, like the mirror in 'Snow White': 'As a lad perhaps my mind was rather narrow, I was innocent and never knew of vice; the thought of girls just shocked me to the marrow; I liked walking and thought kissing was not nice' (almost to the tune of the Policeman's song from Iolanthe); the 14-year-old in the 'Wizard of Oz' who was obliged to confess that his sister comes from a 'dodgy family with a bit of a reputation'; or the shepherd making romantic overtures to a pantomime sheep! Those who don't get a part will probably be written in somewhere anyway. Village schoolmistress, farmer, local dentist, milkman, MP, busybody. No one is above satire.

The Nag's Head Inn becomes a shop and the village gains a temporary cross as preparations are made to film 'Inspector Lynley Mysteries' in 2001.

THE BOOK OF EDALE

EDALE ON SCREEN

Since Universal Pictures Ltd visited Edale in October 1966 to film 'Charlie Bubbles' the valley has been a location for both feature film and television. 'Charlie Bubbles', starring Albert Finney, Billie Whitelaw, Liza Minnelli and Colin Blakely, was filmed mainly in Upper Booth at the home of Miss Greta Shirt. Her house, a former farmhouse dating back to 1580, provided an idyllic location for the film. Other productions include television dramas 'Hideaway', 'Inspector Lynley Mysteries' and 'Far From the Madding Crowd'.

Bottom right: *'Coronation Street's' Albert Tatlock and Gerry Booth outside the Nag's Head Inn as they embark on the Pennine Way in an episode in the early 1970s.*

Below left: *Television personalities Brendan Quayle, Mike Harding and David Bellamy during a break from filming in Grindsbrook Meadows, Edale, in 1994.*

Chapter Nine
SPORTS

Edale has a thriving tennis and bowls clubs and a football team to be proud of. From the late 1800s until 1959 the village also had a cricket team, with its own pitch and pavilion on what is now Cooper's camp-site. In its day, Edale cricket team played against most of the villages in the valley, as well as teams from Rotherham and Sheffield. Sadly, the club is no more. But some day, perhaps… well, who knows?

EDALE CRICKET CLUB

The cricket club was probably formed in the 1880s when there was an influx of workers in Edale during the building of the Midland Railway and Cowburn Tunnel. Photographs of the 1905 team, with Edale Church in the background, confirm that cricket was played on the field behind Cooper's Café, and this field continued to be used until the club closed at the end of the 1959 season.

The cricket pitch had been properly laid at some time prior to 1920 and was protected when not in use by removable posts and chains to keep animals away. The practice pitch was re-laid in December 1921 at a cost of £3.75. The pavilion was converted from an old tramcar body giving a changing area with lockers, seats and a score box. There were seats around the exterior of the pavilion and a toilet area over a stile in the adjoining field. Refreshments were provided in Cooper's Café at the village end of the field.

Each season began with the annual general meeting in early spring when the president, captain, committee and secretary were appointed. During the playing season, committee meetings were held in the Nag's Head on Wednesday evenings. The appointed time for such meetings was 9p.m., but because of farming commitments, and because some members called in at the Church Hotel on the way, meetings did not get started until about 10p.m. Prior to the Wednesday meetings some members spent time on the practice cricket pitch improving batting and bowling and encouraging new members.

The Wednesday meeting was necessary to arrange and pick the team for the Saturday match. This was not easy as several members were farmers and if Saturday proved to be a fine day (a haymaking day) they would not be available. Consequently, No. 11 was often A.N. Other. However, they usually managed to make a team on Saturday by asking any suitable spectator to make up the numbers and this was when juniors were recruited and were able to demonstrate their ability.

During Tom Rowbottom's period as secretary in the 1950s many members played a very active part on the committee. They kept the club going, and without them it could not have survived. They were: Ron Angus, Alan Chapman, Brian Cooper, Edward Cooper, James Cooper, Norman Cooper, Tony Jackson, Vic Noblett, Robert Rodwell, John Rowbottom, Fred Rowbottom, Ted Seyd, Bill Sims and Tom Rowbottom.

Home and away matches were arranged with other Hope Valley clubs, whilst many of the Sheffield clubs had no ground and were pleased to arrange matches at Edale. Some of the fixtures during the period 1935–59 were with: Castleton, Bamford, Hathersage, Grindleford, Tideswell, Calver, Earles, Hayfield, Derwent/Ashopton, Sale, Sheffield Casuals, Sheffield Municipal Officers, Frecheville Meths, Park Congs, Owlerton Church, Rotherham St Peters, YMCA, Sheffield Cathedral, British Aicheson, and the Blood Transfusion Service.

Financially the club was kept viable by members' subscriptions and donations. Interested local residents also gave donations. Whenever new equipment or repairs were required, a whist drive and dance would be arranged with a view to raising the necessary funds. Smaller amounts were raised through collections at matches. Jack Tym, who was one of the regular spectators and acted as umpire occasionally, volunteered his services to collect money whenever he saw an opportunity. It is interesting to note the difference in subscriptions and costs between 1921 and 1959:

	1921	1928	1933	1948	1959
Playing members' subscriptions	£0.25	£0.25	£0.25	£0.38	£0.50
Ground Rent	£5.00	£5.00	£5.00	£5.00	£5.00
Groundsman's Fees	£4.25	£5.00	£5.00	£10.00	£15.00
Cricket Bat	£2.00	£1.75	£1.50	£3.75	£4.00
Cricket Ball	£0.60	£0.60	£0.40	£1.10	£1.00

Edale cricket team, 1900. Left to right, back row: Tom Tym, Len Birch, ?, John Rowbottom, ?, Robert John Cooper; middle row: Joe Noblett, Jim Carrington, Bob Chapman; front row: A. (Tant) Chapman, ?, ?, ?.

Edale cricket team in 1905. Left to right, back row: ?, ?, Harold Shirt, William Sims, Joe Noblett, Revd Harkness, Hives Barber (Nag's Head publican); front row: ?, Issac Cooper, John Rowbottom, Arthur Rowbottom, Robert Chapman.

SPORTS

Edale cricket team in 1911. Left to right, back row: Umpire, Issac Cooper, Harold Shirt, Fred Brown, John W. Rowbottom, Arthur Rowbottom, Robert Chapman, Sam Marrison; front row: Hives Barber, Robert Cooper, William Sims, John Rowbottom, Hector Barber.

Edale cricket team in 1921. The team was made up of members of only two families. Left to right, back row: Joe Cooper (senr), Percy Cooper, Arthur Rowbottom, John W. Rowbottom, umpire, Fred Rowbottom (umpire), Charles Cooper, Richard Cooper, John Rowbottom; front row: Issac Cooper, Edward Cooper, James Cooper, Robert Cooper, Joe Cooper.

Above: The cricket team and opponents, c.1950s.

Left: Fred Rowbottom and family at a cricket match, 1930.

Edale cricket team, 1953. Left to right, back row: Bill Sims, Vic Noblett, Alan Chapman, Robert Rodwell, John Rowbottom, Tom Rowbottom, Edward Cooper; front row: Roy Scott, Joe Mallinson, Cliff Evans, Tony Jackson.

SPORTS

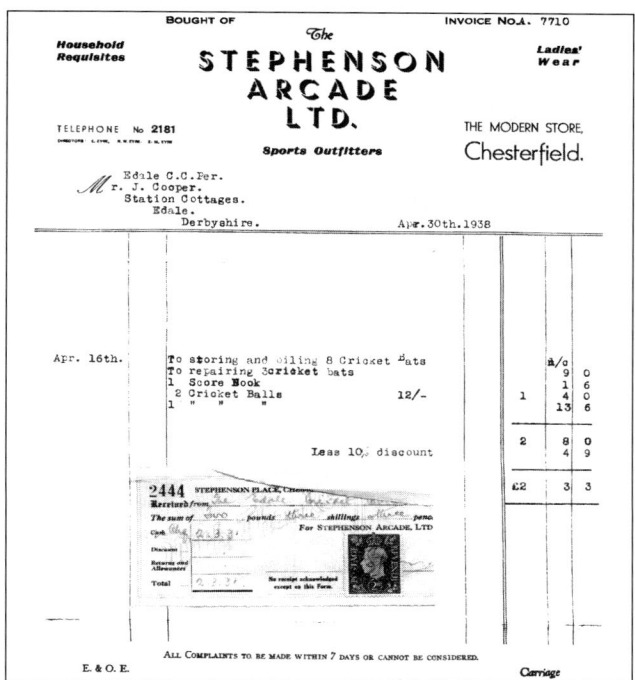

Edale Cricket Club – a bill for storing and oiling bats.

Until 1950 the playing pitch and surrounds were mown with a hand mower but during that year a second-hand ATCO motor mower was purchased for £20. This proved rather expensive to maintain and in 1953 a new Qualcast motor mower was bought for £48. Isaac Cooper carried out ground-maintenance duties for many years up until 1951, after which Arthur Lowe, Steve Kay and John Wharton took over the task for varying periods. Later the playing members carried out the ground duties themselves.

The club captains during the years 1948–59 were as follows:

1948	Brian Cooper
1949	James Cooper
1950	James Cooper
1951	Edward Cooper
1952	Edward Cooper
1953	Robert Rodwell
1954	Robert Rodwell
1955	Edward Cooper
1956	Edward Seyd
1957–59	Ron Angus

The post of club secretary during the years 1920–59 was held by:

1920–25	Joe Allen
1926–27	Robert Cooper
1928–30	Harry Scholey
1930–31	James Cooper
1932–34	Fred Hawtin
1935–38	James Cooper
1939–41	Bill Sims
1947	Bill Sims/Vic Noblett
1948–58	Tom Rowbottom
1959	Cliff Evans

Scorers during the years 1930–59 were:

Ted Smith
Norman Cooper
Brian Cooper
Mary Bentley
Tom Rowbottom
Elizabeth Cooper

Sadly, due to lack of support and to the fact that many Edale members were nearing or were at the end of their cricket-playing life, the club was unable to continue at the end of the 1959 season. It could only have resumed if sufficient support and playing members became available. This was not to be, and soon afterwards the cricket field became a camping and caravan site. The following were the last to play cricket for Edale, 1948–59:

Joe Allen	Joe Mallinson
Ron Angus	David Marrison
Peter Atkin	Peter Noblett
Robert Atkin	Vic Noblett
James Carrington (junr)	Alec Prior
Alan Chapman	Philip Prior
Brian Cooper	Robert Rodwell
Clifford Cooper	Fred Rowbottom
Edward Cooper	John Rowbottom
Eric Cooper	Tom Rowbottom
James Cooper	Frank Richards
Norman Cooper	Roy Scott
Brian Chedlow	Peter Scott
Keith Dakin	Fred Sims
Clifford Evans	William Sims
Arnold Eyre	Edward Seyd
Peter Harris	John Tym
Tom Harris	John Wharton
Alf Harrison	Ken Whippey
David Harrison	Eric Whippey
Tony Jackson	George Wilkinson
Brian Winston	

A cricket match on Cooper's camp-site in 1945. The umpire is Fred Rowbottom and the fielder nearest to the camera is Lem Tym.

Edale Football Club

Although there is evidence of a football team in Edale in the early part of the twentieth century, most records refer to the period from 1930 onwards when Edale FC played in the Hope Valley League. Although not successful in achieving honours they did have an impact on the league, particularly at the close of the 1932 season when, after a dismal season, they defeated local rivals Bamford 2–0 in the last game of the season.

Only the week before, title-chasing Bamford had soundly beaten their nearest rivals, Bradwell, and were confident of taking the title. Hawtin and Noblett scored the goals, but the real hero was the Edale goalkeeper who played an inspired game to beat out everything that Bamford could throw at him. So, thanks to the intervention of Edale, Bradwell took the title on the last day of the season.

During this period the team played on land near the Church Hotel – land on which cottages and police houses were built. Later, the land that eventually became the village's main car park and village hall was also used. In 1947 the vicar of Edale, Revd Massey, started a youth club and from this a new football club was born. A field on the opposite side of the road known as the Barn Field was used as the pitch and some young trees on Back Tor were felled to provide the goalposts with an old metal tube as the crossbar. After playing friendly matches for some time the team was admitted to the Bakewell and District League in the late 1940s. The team made up of Edale lads was successful on a number of occasions but finally wound up in the late 1950s.

The Club of the Twenty-First Century

On 4 June 1971, 18 locals met to resurrect the Edale Football Club with a signing-on fee of 15p and a weekly subscription of 5p. Graham Longden (chairman), Gordon Miller (secretary) and Derek Sowerby (treasurer) were elected to organise the club and a start was made on recruiting players. By the following month there was a playing membership of 23. Fund-raising, mainly from 'Country and Western' events in the village hall, provided equipment, including nets, and second-hand shirts were acquired (until sufficient funds were raised to buy new kit).

Affiliation to Derbyshire County FA was followed by the team being accepted into the Hope Valley League, and the first match took place at Edale on 11 September 1971 against Otters from Buxton. A second-hand wooden hut provided basic changing facilities adjoining the pitch. By 1974 awards were being made to players, with a cup for the highest goal scorer going to David Elliott and the award for the most consistent player given to Stan Taylor. The club captain was Bill Duncan. 'Country and Western' dances in the village hall continued to provide much-needed funds and an annual club dinner was also held. In 1976 the club finished runners-up in the D Division of the Hope Valley League and was promoted. A very successful season also saw the club as runners-up in the Dore and Totley Cup.

By the 1977–78 season there was sufficient interest in the club for a reserve team to be formed to play in the D Division, a place created by the promotion of first team the previous year. Socials continued to play a big part in the club and the minute book shows costs of supplies with large quantities of beer at the top of the list!

The club has had mixed fortunes, but in the 2003 season it was promoted to the A Division of the Hope Valley League for only the second time in its history.

The Tennis Club

Few tennis-courts can match the location of the one belonging to Edale Tennis Club, tucked away in a corner of the village sports field. As players 'change ends', their view switches from the dramatic ridge of Hollins Cross and Mam Tor to a sweeping vista of Grindsbrook overlooked by Kinder Scout. No one can be blamed for missing the occasional ball when surrounded by the distraction of scenery such as this.

After the formation of Edale Tennis Club the court was constructed in 1981 at a cost of £4,063. It was

Edale football team, 2003, promoted to A Division of the Hope Valley League. Left to right, back row: S. Gabbott, O. Metcalfe, D. Howe (player manager), G. Porter, L. Holbrook, G. Maguire, A. Denial, D. Hallam; front row: L. White, B. Eyre, D. Sowerby (assistant manager), D. Gartside, K. Bland, D. Teather. Players missing from photo are S. Shaw, C. Pickford, J. Vize, M. Loxley, N. Jewel, C. Hampson.

Edale Football Club, c.1920–30.

SPORTS

Edale football team, 1946/7. Left to right, back row: Geo Wilkinson (trainer), Joe Mallinson, Norman Cooper, Tony Jackson; middle row: Alan Chapman, Geoff Noblett, Jim Sheldon; front row: Gordon Noblett, ? Chadwick, Geo Goodwin, Bob Smith, Ronnie Bacon. Ken Tym is in the background.

Edale football team, 1973. Left to right, back row: M. Sowerby, D. Chapman, D. Sowerby, S. Taylor, Andy ?, T. Wilde; front row: W. Duncan, W. Fletcher, D. Elliott, C. Moore, G. Longden.

opened by the Duke of Devonshire in 1982. Funds come from members' subscriptions and a dance held every year in the village hall. There is an annual tournament – the categories being singles, mixed doubles, men's doubles and ladies' doubles.

The 'East West' match, started a few years ago, is a 'friendly' competition between residents living to the east of the road from Grindsbrook Booth to the station, and those living to the west of the road. This informal event has become something of a village institution, with excitement running at fever pitch and cheering being so deafening that the umpire's verdict usually goes unheard.

EDALE INDOOR BOWLS CLUB

Edale Bowls Club began in 1997 following a visit by Edale Women's Institute to a Christmas party at Abney WI, also in the Hope Valley, where bowls were a part of the party activities. The ladies returned with a suggestion to form an Edale Bowls Club. A 30-foot mat was hired from Derbyshire County Council, along with bowls and other accessories. However, the mat had to be returned each week. With the help of grants from High Peak Borough Council and Edale Parish Council, income from a dance organised by locals Lawrence and Ruth Yeardley, and interest-free loans from members, the club was able to acquire its own 45-foot mat, bowls and jack. Unfortunately, the mat had to be reduced to 42 feet due to the size of the village hall.

Two competitions are held during the season, from November to March, for pairs' and singles' games. Team pairs are drawn at random. During the four match years, seven different names have appeared on the two trophies, showing a good spread of winners. The club is very much in the best of Edale traditions – sociable and friendly. And the competition is very good-natured.

Membership is drawn from the whole of the valley, with some members coming from the next village, Hope. Visits are made to other local clubs. Bamford and Abney are usually visited each year with return visits by them to Edale. It is doubtful whether the club will produce world-championship bowlers, but everyone enjoys the evening of bowls.

Left: *The Duke of Devonshire being greeted by Mark Gilbert at the opening of Edale tennis-courts and club in 1982, with chairman John Blunden behind. Completed in September 1981, the courts cost £4,063 with the court preparation work being carried out by local enthusiasts.*

Below left: *Edale football team, 1980s. Left to right, back row: K. Wilkinson, J. Carrington, ?, M. Sowerby, S. Claye, ?, J. Hill; front row: E. Townsend, D. Elliott, D. Chapman, K. Bradwell, ?, D. Sowerby (manager).*

Below: *Edale Tennis Club's 'Wine and Strawberries' social event in 1996.*

Chapter Ten

NATURAL HISTORY

Dominated by the Kinder Scout plateau, Edale is situated in the gritstone/shale part of the Peak District known as the 'Dark Peak'. This is an area of acid soils which contrast starkly with the calcium-rich soils of the limestone 'White Peak'. Although this means it is less rich in flora, the Dark Peak has its own unique character.

The peat-covered plateau, rising to 2,000 feet above the village, is of international importance. Its peat channels, locally known as 'groughs', are up to five metres deep and edged with heather, bilberry and cowberry. Cotton-grass, with its fluffy white tops, waves in the wind and indicates pools of standing water, while the large strawberry-like leaves of cloudberry indicate dry areas on top of the peat 'haggs' (the term used to describe the islands of peat between the groughs).

Damp areas are frequented by wading birds such as golden plovers and dunlins, birds that return here for the summer. Raptors, including merlins and hen harriers, may be seen flying close to the ground, often in search of the numerous meadow pipits or the soaring, singing skylarks.

Britain's smallest mammal, the pygmy shrew, is the most common animal on the plateau but is so shy that walkers rarely see it. In the 1930s the mountain hare was reintroduced for game purposes and can often be seen sheltering from the wind between the peat haggs, particularly in winter when its coat has changed to white. When not grazing the heather and bilberry, the hare is often to be found below the plateau edge amongst the rocks where shelter from predators and the wind make an ideal habitat.

The rocks and streams tumbling from the plateau are also a good place to spot the ring ouzel, sometimes known as the mountain blackbird. Where the bands of gritstone give way to the layers of shale, beautiful, clean, peat- and rock-filtered springs burst

View of Grindsbrook Clough and the Kinder plateau from Ringing Roger above the village.

Above: *Grouse in Grindsbrook.*

Left: *A mountain hare changing to its winter white coat during late autumn below Nether Tor.*

out of the hillside providing a rich habitat for sphagnum moss, the main ingredient of the plateau peat. This is interspersed with plants like cranberry, bog asphodel and the insect-eating sundew. Crane-flies and other insects are drawn to these areas and provide mineral supplements to the diet of heather and bilberry eaten by the red grouse, Britain's only indigenous bird.

The grouse has become synonymous with the Peak District moors, and the plateau slopes have been managed for grouse shooting since the late-nineteenth century. The once-wooded valleys leading down off the plateau into the Edale Valley have few relics of that bygone era due to the felling of trees for the lead-smelting industry and for agriculture. Now the slopes are covered not only with heather and bilberry but also with bracken, which is being partially controlled.

As the narrow side valleys have changed, so has the wide shale valley bottom where grass production has been important to farming. Because of its relative isolation, Edale has changed at a slower pace than many other areas and traditional farming practices have meant that some herb-rich meadows have survived to this day. The retention of hedges and drystone walls has also contributed to a diversity of habitats, and most of the typical acid-soil flora can be found there.

Among the drystone walls the occasional stoat or weasel pursues rabbits, while one can also spot badgers, foxes and brown hares. In 1256 mention was made in the accounts of Gervase de Bernake, bailiff of the Peak, of a colt being strangled by a wolf in Edale. Wolves were common in this part of the country at this time and deer roamed freely, as did wild boar. How things have changed!

Chapter Eleven

THE NATIONAL TRUST

The National Trust has been involved in helping to protect the very special qualities of Edale since 1940 – even before the designation of the National Park in 1952. The Trust has gradually extended its protection to include several parts of Edale in a series of 18 acquisitions of varying sizes. As of 2003, the Trust cares for about 38 per cent of the parish and holds these special places on behalf of the nation, forever, for everyone.

The main reasons for all this activity have remained the same: firstly, to ensure that the present and future generations can enjoy the attractive landscape of this delightful Pennine Valley. So much precious countryside has been despoiled by development, the Trust is working hard to prevent undesirable or damaging change in this environmentally sensitive area.

The second aim of the Trust is to help with the conservation of the important and significant features of Edale. This includes not only the natural environment, with its rich heritage of plants, animals and geology, but also the fascinating cultural, historic and human associations within the valley.

A third aim is to ensure that the public at large can benefit from this unique place through the provision of good public access wherever possible. Many National Trust areas in Edale and the surrounding valleys are places of quiet retreat or for education, recreation or exercise away from the exhausting pace of modern life.

Most of these parcels of land in Edale have been acquired with the specific help of members of the public – through many gifts, donations and bequests. This illustrates what a well-loved place Edale is and how successive generations have been anxious to secure its future good health. Public money has also been allocated by successive governments through agencies like the Countryside Commission, for the protection of these parts of Edale for perpetuity.

The policy for Edale is to ensure that most of the National Trust land is looked after, as it has been for thousands of years, by farmers and their livestock. This is because many of the Trust holdings require grazing in order to maintain and manage both their landscape character and the range of wildlife interests, preferably in a sustainable regime with low (if any) inputs of fertiliser and chemicals.

So what does the Trust get up to in Edale? There follow a few examples of the activities in which they are involved.

WINTERING BIRDS

Winter visitors travel thousands of miles to find refuge in Edale. It is a great time of year to look out for flocks of wintering birds like fieldfares and redwings as they wander through the valley. The fieldfare is a favourite. It is a rather attractive thrush which spends the summer in Scandinavia and finds the relatively warm and mild winter climate of the British Isles to its liking. It can be distinguished by its stylish grey rump and noisy flocking behaviour. The fieldfare flocks often also contain a few redwings – again a thrush but with red patches under the 'armpits'. Typically they feed on any berries they can find and the winter landscape of Edale can provide rich pickings in the form of hawthorn bushes bristling with thousands of red haws. Bushes can become totally swamped by ravenous thrushes.

HEDGES

Old mature hedges of the valley are important to wildlife for several reasons. It is often thought that the hedges are mostly used by wildlife in the spring and summer, for nesting and feeding, but good hedges are useful refuelling stations in the winter season too. The best hawthorns for fieldfares are tall and unkempt, some of which may be of considerable age and can support thousands of berries – unlike the closely-cut neat-and-tidy hedges of the roadsides, which look nice but are less useful.

One of the changes that has undoubtedly taken place in Edale this century is the increase in the number of mature unmanaged hedges and trees that have been allowed to grow tall. In the twenty-first century the valley is probably a better environment for wintering fieldfares than it has ever been. Years ago hedges had to earn their keep by acting as windbreaks and stock-proof field boundaries. They were kept stock-proof and neat by laying, the periodic partial cutting and layering of stems. As this practice has become uneconomic in many places hedges have matured and become 'gappy', ending up as just a few hawthorn trees in a line across the field.

This poses a dilemma. On the one hand there is a need to leave as many mature hedgerow trees as possible; on the other hand, historic hedge lines need

The History of the Trust's Presence in Edale Parish

Year	Area (Acres)	Location	How Acquired
1940	346	Lee and Orchard	Gifts by Mrs G.G. Haythornthwaite and Mr A.B. Ward
1942	91	Edale End Farm	Anonymous gift
1943	37	Lord's Seat	Bequest by Mr and Mrs A. Guyler
1945	55	Losehill	Sheffield and District Federation of the Ramblers' Association in memory of G.B.H. Ward
1959	415	Nether Moor (as part of the Hope Woodlands acquisition)	Transferred with Hardwick Hall through National Land Fund procedures
1971	232	Hardenclough	The Hall Fund
1972	71	Small Clough	The Hall Fund
1976	174	Dalehead	Peak District Appeal (PDA), Countryside Commission
1978	14	Dore Clough	PDA, Countryside Commission
1978	75	Upper Clough and other land	PDA and bequests
1981	124	Upper Booth Farm	PDA and Countryside Commission
1981	10	Rushup Edge	PDA
1982	790	Jacob's Ladder, The Cloughs and part of Crowden Brook (as part of the Kinder estate)	National Heritage Memorial Fund Mr Maurice Fry and many individual gifts
1986	23	Northern part of Mam Tor	Countryside Commission, PDA, Mr Raymond Dancey
1987	58.5	Greenlands Farm	PDA, Countryside Commission, bequests x4
1990	15	Lane Head Fields	PDA
1997	45	Ollerbrook covenants	Mrs Caroline Noel
1997	60	Carrington Bank	PDA and bequests
TOTAL	2635.5		

restoration by planting to ensure their future survival – and the old thorns often get in the way. Usually it is extremely difficult to 'lay' old hawthorns as they break easily and don't respond well to being chopped. The best way of re-incorporating a tree into a restored hedge line is to cut or coppice the stem at ground level, forcing it to sprout new stems. However, the usual solution is to combine both methods – to plant new hawthorns in the gaps and coppice a few old trees, but also leave some veterans to provide nectar, habitat and berries for winter bird food.

The Trust has been doing this in Edale since 1978. So far they've planted around 1,500 metres of hedges with the support of the local Peak District members' centre and the Environmentally Sensitive Area scheme (ESA). It is usually costly (£6–10 per metre) as the young plants need protection from nibbling rabbits, sheep and cattle. This means erecting a double fence and possibly tree guards. Another tranche of new hedges is to be undertaken in 2003 at Upper Booth with the help of farm tenants Robert and Sarah Helliwell, members and the agency responsible for the Environmentally Sensitive Area. So, hopefully millions of delicious berries can be produced to sustain and attract our feathered visitors from the north.

Bringing Back the Purple Heather.

Developments in farming have also resulted in landscape change. One of the biggest ecological changes in the British uplands since the Second World War has been the increased numbers of hungry sheep on the hills. The rise in production has been encouraged by government policy and subsidy and our farmers have responded efficiently to the challenge. The drawback has been that many of the sensitive moorland dwarf shrubs have been grazed out, leaving less palatable grasses in many areas. The effect can be seen on some of the grass-dominated moors in and around Edale. The Trust and many farmers are hoping to progressively reverse this trend by restoring heather and bilberry on some of the 'yellowy' hillsides in and around Edale, simply because it is considered better for wildlife and the landscape.

Heather seeding has been carried out on Mam Tor and it is possible to see the benefits of this as the heather and bilberry near Mam Nick expand and develop under an appropriate grazing regime. However, the most extensive project is on Kinder, where the Trust has been working since 1983, in places like the Cloughs (beside Jacob's Ladder), to restore the health of the moor by reducing sheep numbers and encouraging active shepherding. Ironically, the Trust and other landowners and farmers now receive grants from the government to restore these areas – mainly from the North Peak Environmentally Sensitive Area (ESA) scheme, which includes the Edale Valley.

New Roofs for Old Barns

The farming of the moors is inextricably linked with what happens below in the fields and walled landscape – and, critically, at the farmstead with its array of buildings and fields. In a normal year, the Trust team of four builders re-roofs at least three or four buildings on its High Peak estate. The jobs completed by the Trust at the beginning of the twenty-first century in Edale included a large barn at Harden Clough and a new gable-end wall and re-roofing of a barn at Lee House.

All being well, stone roofs usually only require major attention once every 100–200 years or so. The problems can include the stone slates deteriorating (some may 'perish'), the fixings disintegrating, or the timber beneath needing replacement.

Whenever a roof needs repair or replacement, there is always a need for extra stone slates. These are not easy to come by, with the demand high and availability low. The price is therefore costly – at the time of writing slates fetch around £360 per tonne. It takes around one tonne of stone to weatherproof a mere four square yards of roof! With one roof needing on average 20 tonnes of slates and sometimes more – and the skilled labour to put the roof back together again – this is an expensive task. The subscriptions of National Trust members are largely paying for this work and helping to conserve the wonderful heritage of barns and traditional buildings in the Peak District.

As many stone slabs as possible are recycled, but even so some 50 per cent of the original roof or more may be unusable. One of the main problems is finding suitable sources of traditional materials for doing the repairs. As regards slates, second-hand stone is purchased, mainly because it is no longer available locally as newly quarried material.

The Trust's policy is to maintain and conserve all of the buildings that they currently have standing. 'Conserving' means trying to ensure that as much of the original fabric and as many of the original features are preserved for as long as possible, in order to keep the historic character and appearance of the buildings. Because many, unfortunately, no longer have a modern agricultural use, there is a keen desire to find new uses for old buildings – providing that the new use is in keeping and sympathetic to its historic and architectural character. For example, a number have been converted to new accommodation or workshops.

There is a desire to return to the development of the original small-scale 'borrow-pit' quarries from which the right local stone can be sourced, otherwise it becomes a question of 'robbing Peter to pay Paul'. Most of the stone comes from redundant buildings but there is not an inexhaustible supply and new stone will be needed one day. Possibilities for reopening two slate quarries are being investigated by the National Park Authority.

Above: *Lee Farm and Cottage, Upper Booth.*

Below: *General view of the upper Edale Valley towards Jacob's Ladder.*

Opposite, centre: *Eroded scree slope by the packhorse route at Jacob's Ladder, which was restored by the National Trust in around 1985.*

THE NATIONAL TRUST

Mystery at Dale Head

Mundane roof repair is not the only work occupying National Trust builders. In June 2003 a bizarre piece of damage occurred at Dale Head, a converted farmhouse at the top end of the Edale Valley which is used as a hostel for Trust volunteers. One sunny, bright Sunday afternoon, a group of residents returned to find two smashed windows, mysteriously on opposite sides of the front room. Nothing was missing, so was it a burglary? Detective work soon revealed some conclusive evidence: a set of hoof prints and some wool on the glass!

Evidently a sheep had seen its reflection in the window, taken a dislike to this strange animal and decided to head-butt the intruder to its patch. Of course, having leapt at the window it smashed and gave way – the sheep must have bounded into the room like some stunt animal from a James Bond film. Imagine its surprise and panic to find itself inside a darkened room. What did it do? Well it didn't stop, but in a few short strides headed straight for the next bit of blue sky and bounced right out of the window on the other side of the room!

One suspects that the sheep may have had a bit of a headache but it was otherwise unhurt. It can only be hoped that she has learned her lesson! This is one of Edale's greatest mysteries – how can lambs, which are so cute and cuddly, grow up to be as stupid as sheep?

Another Brick in the Wall

Another major part of the Trust's restoration and maintenance work is drystone walling. They employ a team of expert drystone wallers and a number of contractors to do this work. In every square yard of wall there is about one tonne of stone – and it takes a day's hard work to rebuild between one and three metres! On the High Peak estate, 33km of drystone walls have been restored.

Paving the Way

Edale Valley is extremely popular with visitors. They have many positive impacts but also bring one or two problems that have to be addressed on Trust property.

On many occasions National Trust wardens have been stopped and asked by both visitors and a few locals: 'What are those white blobs up on the skyline of Mam Tor, on Jacob's Ladder or the edge of Kinder above Edale? Has it been snowing?' Usually the answer is 'No, they're bags full of stone for footpath repair work.' At the time of writing a moorland paths project has just been completed, largely funded by a £215,000 grant from the Sports Lottery Fund to repair major routes across the Trust's High Peak moors and at Longshaw. The techniques used have been varied – from stone pitching, which is like laying a drystone wall into the path, to 'causey' or flagged paths. Both are traditional methods that were used in the past. Whatever the route chosen, the materials have to be taken to the site – only rarely is suitable stone found close to the job. This nearly always means that a helicopter has to be used to airlift the stone.

This may seem extravagant, but there really is no other way. The alternative would be to spend weeks and months trailing back and forwards across steep and fragile moorland with all-terrain vehicles. Not only would this be more costly, it would also be far more environmentally damaging, and the mess would be much worse than the eroded paths themselves – whereas helicopters are fast, efficient and deliver materials to within a few inches of where you want them. The helicopters usually have a relatively small payload – the biggest up to a tonne or 500 bags of sugar – so the white bags designed for use in the building industry are ideal for loose stone.

Over the years the National Trust and the National Park's Pennine Way Team have lifted from a range of places in Edale – most recently around the Tips car park at Barber Booth. Finding good places to fly from is a problem. It is necessary to get as close as possible to the moorland to minimise flying time, but there is also a need to have good access for delivery lorries. Helicopters too are fussy in their requirements: no trees, no electricity pylons and preferably no buildings! Although there is regret at the noise and inconvenience sometimes caused, there is a strong belief that it is worth it in order to address some of the horrendous footpath erosion problems around the valley.

The aim is not to necessarily make life easy for walkers – far from it – but to provide a hardened, sustainable surface that protects the surviving moorland from further damage. Anyone who has had to struggle through knee-deep, sticky wet peat on the tops will know that such precious habitats are very soft and fragile. Similarly, the 3–4,000-year-old archaeological remains on Mam Tor are delicate and without protection would be lost within a very short period of time. Hopefully, the surfaced paths can provide a compromise solution enabling walkers to visit some of the special places in Edale without causing irreparable damage to the fabric of the landscape they have come to enjoy.

Young Cyril Jackson, son of Eber Jackson (Edale Mill manager) and Louise Jackson, dressed as a soldier during the First World War.

Above: Left to right: *Pat Gilbert (later Atkin), Monica Gilbert and Doreen Gilbert, 1933.*

Audrey Gilbert, Mr and Mrs Issac Broome and Cedric Gilbert in around 1953.

Chapter Twelve

EDALE FAMILIES

People come, and people go, but Edale has been left with a particularly interesting mixture. Some families have been in the valley for centuries. Most of these are – or were – farmers, whose land and livelihood has been handed down from generation to generation. Other families arrived in the nineteenth century to work at Edale Mill, or to build the Midland Railway line and the Cowburn Tunnel. More recently, a regular train service into Sheffield and Manchester has made it possible for many to live in Edale and to work elsewhere.

Whatever the reason for coming to Edale, there has been a tendency for families to stay. The histories of some of these families are included here, but the list is by no means comprehensive.

THE BARBER FAMILY

The Barber family name appears, with a variety of spellings, throughout the history of the High Peak district of Derbyshire. The earliest record found is of a Richard le Barbur (born c.1260), whose wife Margaret is recorded as suing a John Carbonel for her dower in Brocktor, Peak Forest, in 1283.

The Barber family appears to have prospered in the High Peak and in the years c.1399–1413 there are records of Barber family fees paid in the 'Forest of Peak', as shown below. Note that 'Heydall' is believed to refer to Edale, which was also referred to as Edall, Eadall, Edoll and Eydall in documents of the fifteenth to seventeenth centuries:

Edward Barbur for Hassop, 8s.
Edward Barbur for Roole, £4 3s 4d.
William Barbur and Thomas Hagh for Wisden, £6 13s 4d.
John and Richard Barbur for a booth in Heydall (no figure).
John Barbur, Thomas Hall and Ellis Newton for a booth in Heydall, £9 13s 4d

Tradition has it that Lord Grey took men from the parish of Hope to the Battle of Agincourt in 1415. Certainly a Roger Barbour is listed as being on the retinue of Lord Grey.

By 1471 the family fortunes appear to have taken a turn for the worse as Arnold Barbur was accused of stealing, from Castleton, the horse of Robert Townrowe, worth 13s.4d. Later that year the same Arnold Barbur was accused of stealing two more horses, this time from William Townrowe. Around the same time an Edward Barber was accused of stealing a horse worth 10s. from a Richard Smyth.

By the sixteenth and seventeenth centuries, family wills show that branches of the Barber family appear to have settled in the Edale booths of Whitmorley (later known as Barber Booth), including 'Shawood Farm' (Shaw Wood), Grymsbroke (Grindsbrook) and Crowdenley (Upper Booth), as well as owning pasture in 'Ellerbroke' (Ollerbrook) and 'Neder Booth' (Nether Booth). In the Manor Rolls of Castleton for 1522–53 the name of Roger Barber appears as a 'Forester of Fee of Edale and Ashop' and deputy to Sir Rauf Shirley, the Castellon of Peveril Castle. He is later recorded as deputy for John Meverell. By 1567 a Roger Barbour is recorded as deputising for John Meverell's heir.

In 1577, Sir Francis Leek's *List of Alehouses, Inns and Taverns in Derbyshire* records that Guy Barber was 'the keeper of the one alehouse in Eadall'. This would be what is now the Old Nag's Head in Grindsbrook. The family link with the inn continued and a photograph dated 1906 shows the name of Hives Barber over the door.

At some point in the 1600s the booth of Whitmorley started to become know as Barber Booth, in recognition of the Barber family holdings there. This is confirmed in the will of Giles Barber, which was proved in November 1657, whereby 'Giles Barber of Barberbooth, co. Darby' bequeathed 'all my land in Edoll, co. Darby, to William Barber my brother.' Even though no Barber family members live in Edale today, their name remains as a lasting legacy.

The Nag's Head around 1920.

The Barbers of Grindsbrook

```
Thomas Barber of Grymsbroke and Whitmorley (d.1575) = (1) ?   (2) Helene
        ┌──────────┬────────┬────────┬────────┬────────┬────────┐
     Rycharde   Thomas   Edwarde   Ann   Helene   Roger   Jane = John of Crowdenley Booth
                          m.?
              ┌──────────────────┬──────────────────┐
        Francis of Grimesbrook   Rowland of Shawood        Robert
             (d.1633)                (d.1686)
        ┌────────┬────────┐     ┌────────┬────────┬────────┬────────┐
      John = Barbara Creswell  Robert  William   Adam = Ellen  Elizabeth  Ann  Grace  Alles
    (d.1683)                                    (d.1683)
    ┌────────────────┬────────────────┬────────┬────────┬────────┐
Francis of Grindbrook = Elizabeth  John of Neitherhead = Ellen Barber  Adam   Ann  Elizabeth  Mary = Richard Townend   Grace = Hugh Palfreyman
    (d.1713)                                                       (d.1737)                      (Tideswell)                  (Tideswell)
    ┌────┬────┬──────────┬────────┬────────────┬────┬────┬────┐
  Mary  John  Francis = Mary  Joseph   Samuel = Dorothy  Sarah  Ales  John  Joseph
              (d.1742?)                (d.1768)
              ┌──────────────────────────┐
         John Barber of Grinsbrook   Francis Barber of Grinsbrook = Elizabeth
            (d.1968/9)                  (d.1968/9)
                                        ┌──────────┐
                                     Francis     Roland
                                    (bur.1773)  (b.&d.1774)
```

Smith children outside the family shop at Edale Mill Cottages.

EDALE FAMILIES

The Barbers of Whitmorley (Barber Booth) and the Nag's Head

```
                    John Barbur = Eline
                    (will 1535)

  Ralph = Emme Staley    Guy of Nag's Head = Ann   Roland of Ellerbroke   George of Heapfield   Edmund   Joan
  (will 1576)

  Ralph = Margaret  Giles of Heapfield  Elles  8 sisters     Elize   Helen   Amy
  (d.1617)                              (d.1617?)
```

The Barbers of Crowdenley Booth (Upper Booth)

```
              Thomas Barber of Grymsbroke = Helene
              (See The Barbers of Grindsbrook)

  Thomas  Edward  Ann  Helene  Roger  Jane  John of Crowdenley Booth = Margaret
                                            (will 1574)

                                    John Barber    Nicholas of Edall = Joane
                                                   (d.1618)

  Lawrence of Crowden Lee   Robert   Raphe of Crowden Lee = (1) ? (2) Jane     William of Crowdenley and Mellerfoulde = Ann
                                    (d.1690)

  John  Robert    Nicholas = Mary   Ann      Thomas = Emmett    Grace         John of Crowden Lee = Hannah
        (1644–89) (1646–89)         (b.1649) (b.1651)           (d.1648)

                                                                 John          Mary      John
                                                                 (d.1687 age 2) (d.1687)  (1688–99)

  Sarah   Joses     Ann   Sarah      Alles    Joseph  Stephen  Martha  Benjamin = Isabel  Mary        Mary      Samuel
  (d.1678) (1678–82)      (1685–1713) (b.1690) (b.1684)                (1690–1763)        (b.&d.1693) (d.1695)  (b.&d.1696)

                                                      Mary      Benjamin   Elizabeth  Joseph    Thomas    Elles
                                                      (b.1728)  (1734–48)  (b.1730)   (b.1738)  (b.1741)  (b.1744)
```

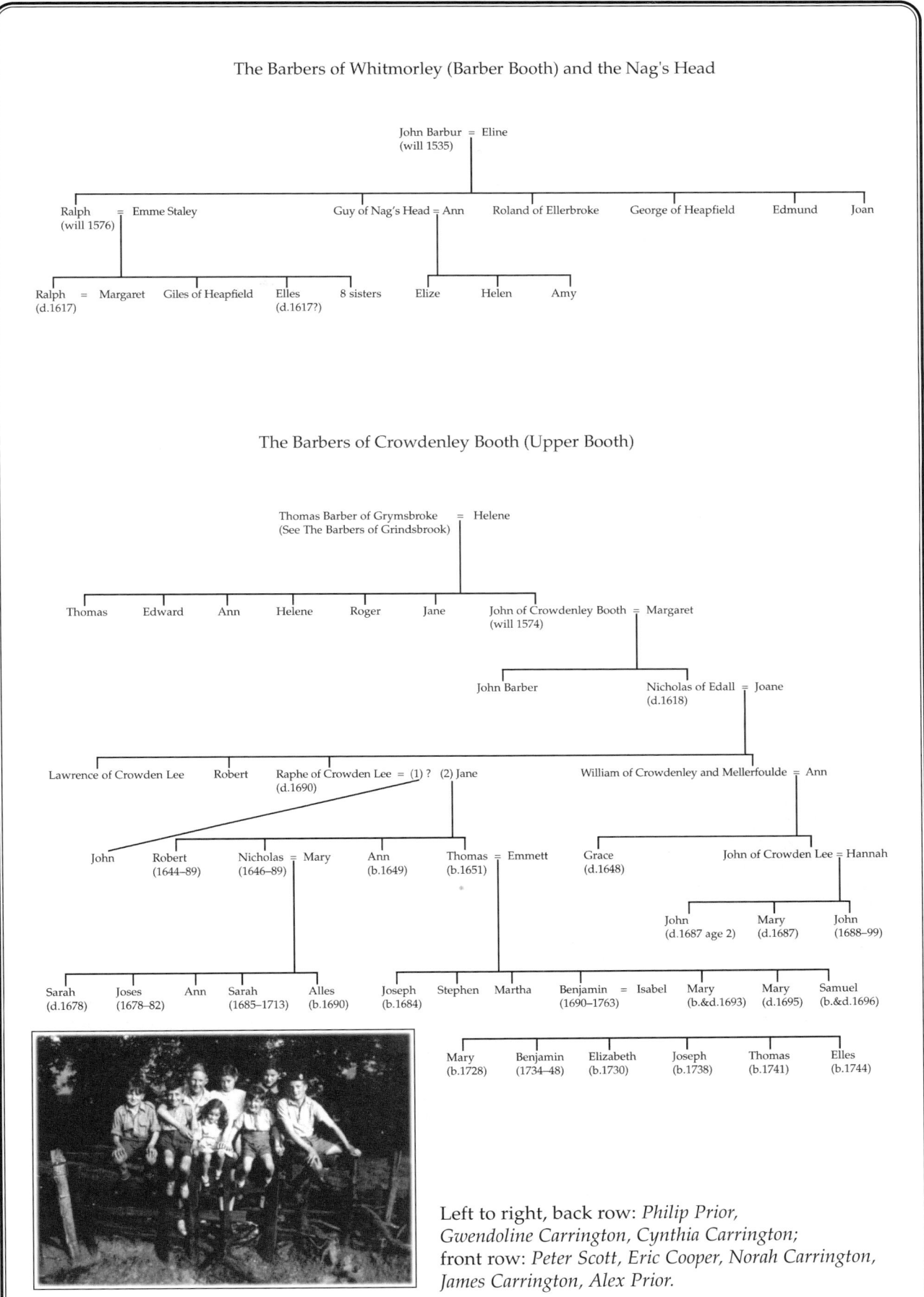

Left to right, back row: *Philip Prior, Gwendoline Carrington, Cynthia Carrington;* front row: *Peter Scott, Eric Cooper, Norah Carrington, James Carrington, Alex Prior.*

139

Left to right, back row: *William Carrington, Margaret Prior;* front row: *Alex Prior, Edith Carrington, James W. Carrington, Cynthia Carrington, James Carrington.*

Left: *The Carrington family in 1946. Left to right: Norah, Cynthia, James D. and Gwendoline Carrington.*

Right: *The grandchildren of Mr and Mrs Critchlow in 1949. Left to right: Norah Carrington, James Carrington, Jean Nield, Christine Eyre, John Nield, Gwendoline Carrington, Cynthia Carrington, Margaret Eyre.*

James Carrington, James D. Carrington and James W. Carrington at Ivy House, Barber Booth, 1949.

The Carrington Family

Whilst some uncertified research places the Carringtons in Edale back to the late-fourteenth century, ratified evidence confirms their presence over nearly 400 years and as such they are the longest-known surviving local family. The family pedigree, which is shown overleaf, begins with James (d.1645) and ends, perhaps fittingly, 300 years later with James David (b.1945). Still living locally at the time of writing, James David owes his life to the prompt actions of his sister Norah and uncle, Jack Prior of Broadlee, Barber Booth. When James was struck by lightning in 1967, whilst working on the land at Ivy House, Jack resuscitated him whilst Norah sought medical help.

James' family came to Edale from Bugsworth in the early-seventeenth century and settled in the area known at the time as Whitmore Lea Booth; changed in the early 1700s to Barber Booth. During the next 250 years much of the land farmed in the area from Whitmore Lea west to Crowden Lea was tended by their descendants. Their 'cousins' lived at Bugsworth Hall and were felt-hat manufacturers in Stockport for a number of generations. (*Yeoman's Home – A History of Bugsworth and its 'Hall'* by James Abson (1981) is a worthy reference.)

The booths (or folds as they were sometimes called) were sited on terraces next to a water-supply and in a good defensive position in order to shelter winter store cattle against wild animals and man. Up to the 1660s all the farmsteads were in booths and their respective lands formed elongated bands, like spokes in a wheel, around the booth. The Carrington wills show how, in common with other families, there was a constant exchange of fields between each other. This practice seems to have gone on for centuries in Edale and to some extent still does!

Throughout their time in Edale the Carringtons have been primarily involved in either farming or other occupations associated with the land. In order to supplement the inadequate income from farming, other work both within and outside the parish of Edale was sought. Examples of such activity is attributed to the last three of the Carrington 'tree' who farmed at 'Ivy House', Barber Booth, from the last quarter of the 1800s up to the end of the twentieth century. For example, Thomas (1816–94) spent a number of years farming in West Yorkshire where he met and married his future wife, Hannah, before returning to farm in Barber Booth; James (1877–1956) sought gardening work and for many years helped at Grindsbrook House; James William (1909–95) was involved in the 'quest for oil' project which was undertaken on land at Whitmore Lea circa 1938.

The Carringtons were a respected family having close links with, or giving strong support to, all the traditional village activities. In particular, the Church of The Holy and Undivided Trinity, the Methodist chapel, the village school, the horticultural society and the cricket and football clubs were high on their list. The 1720 seating list for the chapel shows that William Carrington (b.1690) had a share in two pews.

Whilst routine work (such as the milking and feeding of cattle) was maintained, the sabbath was a day of obligatory abstinence from both work and play in the Carrington household. Accordingly, no member of the family would be found harvesting on this day, however difficult the season's weather might have been.

The old graveyard at Edale has a fitting memorial to a well-loved and respected family member, namely John Bayley Carrington (1814–90): 'In Loving Memory of John Carrington, for many years keeper of the Edale Moors. This cross is erected in recognition of his faithful services and sterling qualities.'

All families have characters and the Carringtons are no exception. There is a story still told to this day, by those old enough to remember. This relates to William (1874–1952) who went on the annual gathering of sheep on East Moor, Longshaw. The tradition was, and still is to some degree, to find the nearest 'watering hole', or inn at the end of the gather. Apparently William stayed until 'throwing out' time and was in an advanced stage of inebriation. As all of the other Edale farmers had gone some time earlier William had no way of getting a lift back home. Fortunately a local farmer was still at the inn and agreed to take on the responsibility. He took William to Grindleford railway station and placed him in the guard's van with a note pinned to him which read 'Put off at Edale'.

In addition to the spiritual link with Edale Methodist Chapel, Ivy House, the family home for over 230 years, stands adjacent to the chapel, which to the time of writing the Carrington family continues to support and regularly attends for worship. Ivy House, which was built in 1765 for Mary and James (1734–76), was the home of the Carringtons (except for a short period) from its construction until 1997.

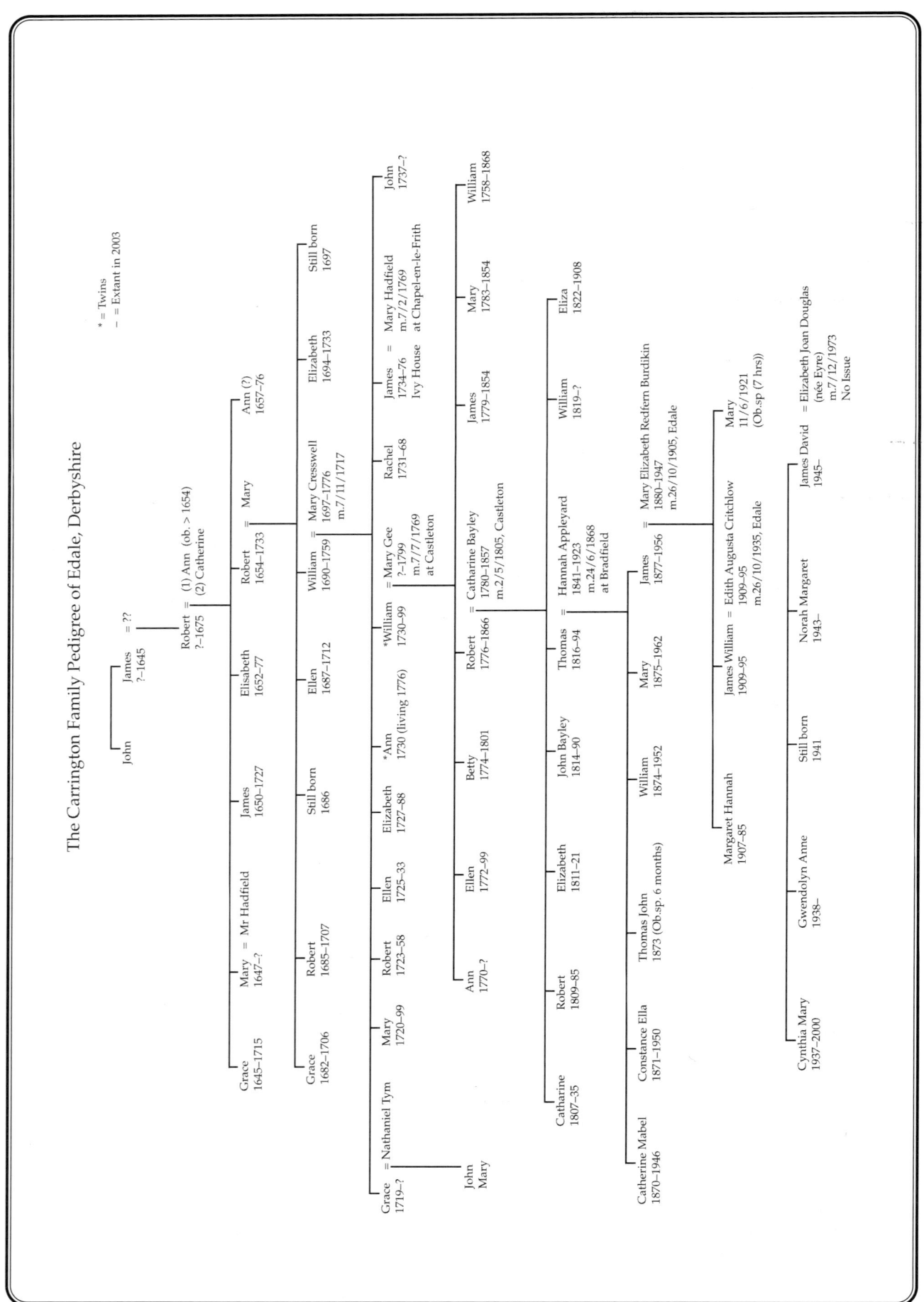

EDALE FAMILIES

Left: *The Prior family at Broadlee, Barber Booth, in 1949. Left to right, back row: Jack Dixon Prior; front row: Alex Prior, Margaret Prior, Philip Prior.*

Right: *The Cooper family outside the old Post Office, c.1917.*

Left: *Edale Post Office, c.1930, before the building of the shop.*

THE COOPER FAMILY

Known in his time as the 'Grand Old Man of Edale', Joseph Cooper died in 1940 in his 90th year. Born into a farming family in Edale, he was well known throughout the area and was one of the earliest traders at Sheffield Market. For many years before the railway opened in 1894, he made the journey to Sheffield by horse and cart, a distance of over 20 miles, collecting farm produce for the market on the way. He would return with food, which he sold from his tiny shop in Grindsbrook Booth. Joseph Cooper was also the first man to fetch coal for the village from Dronfield, when he was often caught in winter snow on the Fox House moors.

Joseph recalled a winter's tale when he was trapped in snow as he entered the Edale Valley through the lofty Mam Nick road on his way back from Chapel-en-le-Frith. Darkness fell and he was still stranded. Down in the valley he could see lights as farmers went about their tasks. He was even able to tell what was happening on his own little farm in the village. He saw a large number of lights leave his home and wend their way to the foot of the hill where he was able to alert the party by waving his lanterns. However, it was still some hours before he returned to the village in triumph. He liked to recall that he had on board a quantity of medicine for some sick cattle in the village and had promised a farmer friend that he would be back as early as possible. Needless to say he arrived just in time to save the cattle.

When the railway opened, bringing with it the more rapid transport of goods, his business increased and the small shop expanded into the company of Joseph Cooper and Sons. Mr Cooper became the first postmaster in Edale, a position he held for 50 years.

After retiring from the Post Office, Joseph and his wife resided at Waterside Farm where they continued to take an active part in the social, sporting and community life of the village. They celebrated over 50 years of marriage and at their golden-wedding party (aged 86 and 76) their eight sons and two daughters were surprised and delighted when their mother appeared in her wedding dress that she had last worn 50 years earlier.

Joseph was a member of the Edale Ancient Order of Foresters and an enthusiastic and inspirational member of the village cricket team. Joseph and his wife died within weeks of each other in the great snow of 1940.

The business has passed on through his sons Percy, Joseph and Edward, granddaughter Elizabeth (postmistress) and in 2003 is still owned and run by grandson Roger and his wife Penny (postmistress). Waterside is still in the Cooper family at the time of writing. A small café was also part of the business and was originally run by Percy's wife, May. The schoolchildren would cross the road each day for her home-cooked dinners, while on Saturdays the village cricket team eagerly awaited her teas at the interval.

A large café was built later, and this was also a popular venue for dances, whist drives, jumble sales

THE BOOK OF EDALE

Above: *Coronation tea in Cooper's Café in 1953.*

Below: *The opening of Cooper's Café extension, 19 May 1950.*

Alice Cooper, wife of Edward Cooper.

144

EDALE FAMILIES

Above: *A provisions cart at Edale Post Office, c.1920s.*

The wedding of Edward and Alice Cooper in 1935.

Edale Post Office in 1930, prior to the building of the café.

Below: *Edward Cooper who lived at the Post Office and also worked at Edale station.*

and for meetings of the Mothers' Union. The local amateur dramatics society regularly held plays and pantomimes in the café extension. In the late 1950s part of the hall was used as a briefing centre for National Park voluntary wardens.

Two of Joseph Cooper's grandsons, Clifford and Eric, provided a taxi service, collecting children from the various booths and taking them to Edale Primary School or to Hope for secondary education. While many members of the family have left the village over the years, they have maintained strong links and James, who started a teaching career as a student teacher in Edale School and went on to become a successful teacher elsewhere, returned to retire in the

Some members of the Cooper and Noblett families on an omnibus outing, c.1930s.

village. At the time of writing the Post Office, café and camp-site are well known to visitors to this beautiful valley and keep the Cooper family name prominent.

THE HADFIELD FAMILY

One of the oldest families in Edale, the Hadfields appear to have taken their name in Saxon times from the villages of Hayfield, immediately to the west of Edale, and Hadfield near Glossop. Although the Hadfields' researched records date from the 1600s, it is believed that the family lived in the valley long before that time. Most of the family wills from the seventeenth and eighteenth centuries refer to the family as 'yeomen' in Whitmorelea Booth. One of these is witnessed by a Robert Carrington. At that time the Crown still owned land in Edale, and Charles I, desperate for money, disposed of land at Crowdenlea (now Upper Booth) and Whitmorelea (now Barber Booth) via middlemen to Ralph Cresswell and Giles Barber. They in turn sold this on almost immediately, including other land bought in 1653, to Thomas Hadfield.

The family name is also found among the 15 'founders' of the first Edale chapel in 1634. In the family history there is mention of support for the Loyalist cause and subsequent suffering following the 'horrors and fanaticism of the Civil War', although other Hadfields seem to have supported the

John Rowbottom in 1937.

John Rowbottom (left) and his father Arthur haymaking in the Lea Barn fields, Grindsbrook Booth, in the 1950s.

EDALE FAMILIES

Norah Rowbottom (on the horse), Margaret Rowbottom (standing), John Rowbottom, Donald Hurst and John Tym (on the hay cart). The Nab can be seen in the background, 1935/6.

Parliamentarians. The Hadfield family had a further impact on religion in Edale when in 1750 John Hadfield became the first member of a Methodist society. Meetings were held in his home, which has since been demolished and replaced by the Methodist chapel which was founded by Joseph Hadfield in 1811.

On 23 February 1889 a John Hadfield was charged with stealing a pair of trousers and jailed for two months. He was not a local, but was employed by a contractor.

At the time of writing there are no members of the Hadfield family in Edale, although a Hadfield is said to buy sheep from the valley each year, so preserving the connection with the valley that goes back to the earliest known records.

THE ROWBOTTOM FAMILY

The Rowbottom family came to Edale in the late 1500s and early 1600s from the area between Glossop and Marple in the counties of Derbyshire and Cheshire. Wills obtained for this period confirm the family origins at Glossop, Mottram, Marple, Mellor and Chisworth.

The first proof of their residence in the Edale Valley comes from the will of Henry Rowbottom who died in Edale in 1622 and was buried in Castleton churchyard. He was born in the Glossop/Marple area c.1550, and his connection with this area was confirmed by the witness and appraiser of the will. He may have moved to Edale as a forester, woodworker, or farm worker, and probably lived at Carr Bank, Grindsbrook.

The next known relative of Henry who came to Edale was John Rowbottom, who was born at Mottram in 1623. He married Mary in 1644 and lived at Carr Bank, Edale. John, with other men in the 1660s, purchased the right to collect rents due to the Commonwealth (formerly of the Crown) in the Edale Valley. These were nominal dues on what was otherwise freehold property, known as 'fee-farm rents'. They reverted to the Crown in 1662.

Following Henry and John to the Edale Valley, descendants settled in the valley and took up farming, carpentry and wheelwright work. The workshop in the Nag's Head Inn yard is mentioned in family wills, and also a section of the family located at Ollerbrook were carpenters and wheelwrights.

The family continued through the 1700s and 1800s as farmers, carpenters and wheelwrights and took up residence at various houses and farms including Carr Bank Cottage, Grindsbrook Cottage, Lea House and Farm, Limefield Farm, The Warren and workshop,

Lea House, Grindsbrook Booth, 1913. **Left to right:** *John Wright Rowbottom with daughter Phyllis, Arthur Rowbottom (the village constable), Issac Cooper with daughter Olive. The stone seen on the left was reclaimed during the building of the school extension.*

Sarah and William Sims.

EDALE FAMILIES

Above: *Margaret Sims with Frederick and Geoff.*

Above: *Ethel Marsh outside Dore Clough Farm, the Sims' family home.*

Right: *Margaret Sims (née Hardy), c.1922.*

Church Cottage, Ollerbrook Cottage, Rose Cottage and Sunnyside.

In relatively more recent times Thomas Rowbottom married Grace Gould of Uttoxeter in 1853 and had three sons and five daughters. Two of the sons, John and Thomas, continued in the family trades, John as a farmer and wheelwright and Thomas as a carpenter and builder.

John (b.1856) had three sons – John Wright, Arthur and Harold. John Wright was a carpenter and wheelwright at The Warren; Arthur took over the farm at Lea House and Limefield; and Harold was a schoolteacher at Buxton, retiring to Edale in later life.

Thomas (b.1862) had two sons – Thomas Henry and Fred. Thomas Henry trained as a plumber but was killed in the First World War, in 1917. Fred was a carpenter and builder and worked from Rose Cottage.

The sons of both Arthur and Fred left the village to find employment elsewhere and no Rowbottoms remain in the village, other than married daughters and their children.

Descendants of the family are now spread around the country and abroad, including Edale, Bradwell, Bamford, Litton, Buxton, Knutsford, Bromley, Solihull, Harpenden and Auckland, New Zealand.

The Sims Family

Frederick Richard Sims (b.1860) and his wife Anne (b.1862), with three young sons, Richard (b.1895) Henry (b.1897) and William (b.1900), arrived in Edale from Bradfield near Sheffield in about 1901. Two more children, Sarah (b.1902) and Dora (b.1906), were born in Edale. The family lived for a short time in Rose Cottage, moving to Higher Hollins from where, in 1910, they made their final move when Frederick purchased Dore Clough Farm, a smallholding of approximately 32 acres.

Frederick, who was born at Wirrall Hall near Sheffield, was one of the best-known gamekeepers in North Derbyshire. For seven years he was in charge of the Bradfield Moors, under the ownership of a Mr C. Skinner of Throapham Manor, Rotherham. He came to Edale when Mr Skinner took over the shooting on the Edale Moors.

In 1919 Frederick had charge of the Edale side of Kinder Scout. His knowledge of grouse was unequalled and his advice was sought by scores of landowners throughout the country. Frederick was a noted shot and on one occasion, when shooting over Bradfield Moors, killed 49 birds without a single miss!

In his youth, Frederick was a noted exponent of 'knur and spell'. He was also a good cricketer and at one time played for the Yorkshire 2nd XI, and later for Edale until he was 60 years of age. Gardening was his hobby, and for 11 consecutive years he won the gardening championship of the Edale Horticultural Society, of which he was a member for 30 years.

Frederick died at the age of 73 and is buried along with his wife in Edale churchyard. Only two of his children, William (Bill) and Henry (Harry), remained in Edale.

Harry's daughter, Dora Yates, who is 80 years of age and a widow living in Yorkshire at the time of writing, tells of the time when she was about ten years old, going with her dad and granddad to build up the shooting butts. When they were shooting she went as gun carrier and earned ten shillings (50p) a day. One year all the whisky and beer stashed near Four Jacks cabin was taken. They never did find it.

Although Harry's main interest was shooting, and he was, by all accounts, a recognised marksman, neither he nor younger brother Bill followed their father into gamekeeping. The one thing they did inherit from him, however, was an interest in gardening, and for many years Bill was also a winner at the Edale Horticultural Show.

Dore Clough eventually became the home of Bill, his wife Margaret, and their two sons Frederick and Geoffrey. In 1978 the farm was sold by auction to the National Trust. Bill and Margaret moved to a pensioner's bungalow nearer the village.

Connections with the Railway

The following is taken from a newspaper cutting from April 1943:

WOMAN POSTED TO SIGNAL BOX.

The first railway signalwoman to be appointed in the Hope Valley is Mrs Dora Yates, whose home is at 17 Hope Road, Edale. The only daughter of Mr & Mrs Harry Sims, Hope Road, Edale. Mrs Yates was married on Wednesday week to Sapper John Terrence Yates, of the Royal Engineers, whose home is in Swinton, Manchester.

Mrs Yates joined the railway service shortly after war broke out, when women were being utilised as porters. She was at Hope station for a long time and then on the relief staff, working at stations between Bamford and Chinley. While working at these various stations, Mrs Yates picked up the idea of becoming a signalwoman and was sent to complete her training at Edale Station Box. She passed the necessary examinations and was then appointed to take charge of the Norman's Bank signal box, between Hope and Edale, where she will carry out exactly the same duties as the men posted at this box.

Mrs Yates' father is employed on the Edale length of the permanent way, an uncle is employed on the Cowburn length of the Dore and Chinley line, an aunt is employed in the booking office at Bamford station and another uncle is a signalman in the Staveley area.

EDALE FAMILIES

Margaret Sims and son Geoffrey at Dore Clough, 1944.

Memories of Dora Yates (née Sims)

Charlie Turner from Sheffield ran Clay Pigeon shoots in the Hope Valley and my dad won a lot of prizes at these events. I still have many of his cups.

One evening during the Second World War someone (Garry Goodwin) accidentally set fire to the cookhouse. [Note: Dora is referring to the soldiers who were billeted at Edale Mill during the war.] *The Germans were flying overhead and, seeing the flames, dropped a landmine. Luckily it missed us but landed in Castleton. We went to look where it had landed and I found a great big piece of Blue John in the road. I still have it.*

As a child I remember swimming in the dam at Edale Mill during long hot summers. The winter was a different thing altogether, very cold and lots of snow. One year the drifts were so bad the railway was blocked at the Edale end of Cowburn Tunnel. Edna Mallinson was taken ill with appendicitis and they had to send a snow plough engine to take her to the hospital in Sheffield. I can also remember when the snow was so deep they had to make a tunnel through the snow to empty a post box!

Granddad always liked to get the hay out of the way before the flower show in August. So Vic Noblett would bring his horse-drawn mower, but they couldn't get near the edges of the field and granddad would have to do them with a scythe. The hay was then turned twice – a long job – then we stacked it in piles to dry before carting it to the barn. We loved to ride on the haycart and drink glasses of Gran's special brew of heather beer.

Most of the girls in the village went into the armaments factory at Bamford during the war. I didn't fancy that, so I asked about the Land Army. There was nothing in Edale, but railway porters were wanted and so I joined the railway. This led to me becoming the first signalwoman appointed in the Hope Valley.

The Tym Family

Only one recorded authority on names mentions the name Tym, and it is thought that it is derived from a Tim or Timothy in the 1300–1400s. By 1560 the name is found at Mottram in Longdendale near to Glossop, at Rotherham and in Dronfield, less than 25 miles from Edale. It seems likely that the Tyms came to the Castleton area in the early 1600s, and in the 1640s a Dennis Tym of Losehill, Castleton, had a child baptised. By 1645 a Tym of Losehill was a tenant of the Brights at Backtor Farm, Edale. It would appear that they then spread through marriage in Edale. In 1653 John and Alice Tym had a son Martin baptised in the chapel at Edale. Although records at this time for Edale were kept in Castleton, there is a lack of registers before 1660.

There are records of a John Tym at Losehill (1667) who was likely to have had connections with a John Tym of Ollerbrook, Edale, who died in 1698. Another Tym, Nicholas (1683–1761), lived at Brocket Booth Farm just over the hill from Edale. The likelihood is that most Tyms in the nineteenth century were descended from these families.

Family tales tell of a Tym connection with Scotland and an inhabitant of Edale at the time of writing, Amy Tym, believes that Tyms left Edale as drovers and moved to Scotland before returning with James I in 1603, when they resettled the area. Descendants of John Tym (1768) still living in the valley at the time of writing are Andrew and Raymond Critchlow; John Nield and his sister Jean Chapman; Amy Tym from Nathaniel's line; and Alan and Paul Tym from Micah and Samuel's lines.

Rowland Cote Farm at Nether Booth, since rebuilt and now the youth hostel and activity centre, was inhabited for many years by Tyms. Shaw Wood Farm has been in continuous occupation by the Tym family and their descendants for centuries.

While demographic changes continue to affect Edale, as in other communities around the country, it is heartening to know that links to Edale's distant past are still maintained in this beautiful Derbyshire High Peak valley.

Edale Families Celebrate

Over the years many celebrations have taken place in the valley. A few of them are recorded here in pictures.

Edale Village Band on coronation day, 1911.

THE BOOK OF EDALE

The wedding of Madge Fitzmaurice, daughter of Mrs R.J. Cooper, head teacher at Edale School for 36 years.

Right: *Edale girls celebrate coronation day, 1911.*

Below: *Coronation day, 1911, outside the Nag's Head Inn.*

EDALE FAMILIES

The 1953 coronation fancy-dress parade in Grindsbrook Booth. Left to right, back row: ?, Fred Sims, Keith Dakin, Marjorie Cooper; middle row: David Harrison, John Jefferies, ?, Jenny Rodwell, Elizabeth Cooper, Joyce Cooper, Jackie Cooper, Ann Richards; front row: Susan Jefferies, Maureen Dakin, Eileen Lowe, Harold Cooper, ?, Brian Richards, ?, Roger Cooper.

EDALE Coronation Celebrations
JUNE 2nd, 1953.

Programme of Events.

✝

SUNDAY, MAY 31st,

THE PARISH CHURCH,

Services at 10-0 a.m. and 7-0 p.m. will be specially adapted to the occasion of the Coronation.

CORONATION DAY, TUESDAY, JUNE 2nd.

Television will be installed in the School and will operate during the B.B.C's. transmissions.

2-30—5-0. Children's Sports in Cooper's Field.

4-0 onwards. Adult's Tea in Cooper's Café.

5-0. Children's Tea in Cooper's Café.

5-45. Presentation of Scholars' Souvenirs in the Schoolroom by the Vicar.

6-30. Fancy Dress Parade for Judging in the Square.
    Class 1. Children up to and including 7 years.
    " 2. Children, 8 to 15 years inclusive.
    " 3. Pedestrians (16 years and over), prams, cycles, push-carts and motor cycles.
    " 4. Lorries, cars, tractors, horse drawn vehicles and trailers.

7-30. Fancy Dress Tour of Valley.

7-30 onwards. Music in the Village Field.

9-30. Dance in the School.

11-0. Lighting of Bonfire on Lords Seat.

Edale children celebrate the coronation of Queen Elizabeth II in 1953. Left to right, back row: Keith Dakin, Philip Prior, Marjorie Cooper, Gwen Carrington; third row: Edmund Howe, ?, David Harrison, Peter Scott, Sally Seyd, ?, John Nield, Eric Cooper; second row: Elizabeth Cooper, Roger Cooper, James Carrington, John Jefferies, Norah Carrington, Brian Allsop, ?, Jenny Rodwell, Robert Rodwell; front row: Rosemary Dalton, Eileen Lowe, Carol Howe, Ann Richards, Rachel Tomlinson, ?, Brian Richards, Geoff Sims, Susan Jefferies.

The Jackson brothers Morgan and Simon from Edale share the same wedding day on 10 September 2000 at Edale Church. Left to right: Stacey Fielding, Morgan Jackson, Andreijana Maksimovic, Simon Jackson.

Right: *Tony Favell, Richard Code and Amy Tym enjoy the golden jubilee celebrations in the village hall.*

EDALE FAMILIES

Edale Brownies on silver jubilee day, 1977. Left to right: *Mandy Oakes, Fiona Harrison, Emma Giles, Julia Nichols, Elaine Whiteley, Elizabeth Gilbert, Jane Widdowson, Tania Wetherall.*

Edale Country Day on the Village Hall Field, 2003.

Above: *Golden jubilee celebrations in the village hall, 2002. Left to right:* Amy Tym, Lyn Widdowson, Ruth and Lawrence Yeardley, ?, Clive Wetherall, Alice Helliwell.

Above: *Coronation Parade, 1911. The men with sashes are members of the Edale Ancient Order of Foresters.*

Right: *Cycle race at Edale during the coronation celebrations in 1911.*

EDALE FAMILIES

The Edale Valley makes a beautiful background for the village photograph taken at the golden jubilee celebrations in 2002. Left to right, back row: John Shirt, John Gee, John Greenlees, John Tupholme, David Shirt, David Worthington, David Shirt junr, Pauline Shirt, Ben Skillern, Geoff Townsend, Tony Evans, Jill Harrison, Michael Wilson, Raymond Critchlow, Mark Reeves, Richard Grimes, Jayne McGivern, Nigel Green, Stephen Searle; fifth row: Lynda Shirt, Cedric Gilbert, Isobel Greenlees, John-Henry Ballantyne, James Ballantyne, Kathryn Reid, Julia Reid, Joanna Reid, Luke Archer, Theresa Skillern, Mark Skillern, Morgan Jackson, David Hove, Samantha Reeves, David Crossland, Steve Wilson, Chris Hemsley, Graham Mountford, Joy Searle; fourth row: Andrew Favell, Val Gilbert, Sarah Gee, Sally Gee, Diane Shirt, John Atkin, Sandra Atkin, Elizabeth Archer, Jane Archer, Nancy Evans, Jane Beney, Alan Chapman, David Baird, Julia Belton, David Belton, Gordon Miller, Fiona Hendry, Carol Wilson, Margaret Mountford, Victoria McKeon, Andrew Critchlow, Anita Critchlow, Derek Soverby, Robin Metcalfe, Steve Trotter, Jo Trotter, John Connors, Glynis Ballantyne, Hannah Rumble, David Wilson, Greg Erskine, Joan Bower, Ashlin Bower, Paula Gilbert, Tony Gilbert and Jake, Joe Hardy, Beth Hardy, Rob Jackson, Bella Hardy, Emma Hardy, Jan Hardy, Anne Barnes, Nicola Wood, Robin Wood; third row: Elizabeth Wetherall, Michael Ballantyne, Clive Wetherall, Fairlie Elrington, Tony Favell, Sue Favell, Jean Rodwell, Muriel Shirt, Roy Cooper, Gaven Cooper, Lyn Widdowson, Milly (Nancy) Heardman, Jean Chapman, Dorothy Baird, Lawrence Yeardley, Ruth Yeardley, Harry Newton, Mary Elliott, Roger Neves, Barbara Neves, Norah McKeon, Terry McKeon, Helen Metcalfe, Diane Metcalfe, John Earl, Michael Barnes, Rosie Rumble, Katharine Bagshaw, Paul Lorrigan, Sarah Helliwell, Robert Helliwell, Jenny Rodwell, Elizabeth Gilbert, Peter Scanlon, Josie Scanlon, Jill Neves, Austin Neves; second row: Alan Atkin, Pat Atkin, Belinda Critchlow, Joan Williams, John Nield, Lindsey Gilbert, Julie Morton – Edward and Hannah, Brenda Oakes, Morris Oakes, Paula Greenlees, Denise Thwaites Bee, Julian McIntosh, Amy Tym, Lesley Code, Carole Hemsley, Alex Hemsley, Gisella Glanville and Dominic, Horace Jackson, Pauline Jackson, Margaret Connors, Carol Jamieson, Johnny Yeoman, Hilary Yeoman, Caroline Jackson, Emma Neves-Love, Chris Bowns and Reuben, Berlie Doherty, Alan Brown, Angela Quigley, Terry Dannery; front row: Alice Helliwell, Emma Greenlees, Grace Dannery-Quigley, Alice Dannery-Quigley, Holly Thwaites Bee, Joy Shand, Rowan McIntosh, Aimée Code, Richard Code, Josephine Code, Freya Scott, Stephanie Reid, Jonathan Glanville and Kristian, Cassie Wild, Liam Turner, Ollie Wood, Ellen Helliwell, Jo-Jo Wood, Callum Critchlow, Emerson Mountford, Frazer Mountford, Jake Neves-Love, Louis Neves-Love, Harry Neves-Love, Elspeth Critchlow, Harris Mountford, Genevieve Gilbert, Richard Worthington, Shane Townsend, William Hove.

Subscribers

Corean M. Atkin, Edale, Derbyshire
Katharine E. Bagshaw, Edale, Derbyshire
Mary E. Bailey (née Critchlow), Holt, Wrexham
Mrs A. Barber (née Hornsby), Brampton, Cumbria
Anne Barnes, Edale, Derbyshire
Marjorie Lillian Beard (née Cooper), Cumbria
Holly M.T. Bee, Edale, Derbyshire
Jane Beney, Edale, Derbyshire
Bentley
Anne Boff, Bottesford, Nottingham
Joan and Ashlin Bower, Edale, Derbyshire
Prof F.M. Burdekin, Bollington, Macclesfield
Wendy Butcher, Edale, Derbyshire
James D. Carrington, Bamford, Derbyshire
Tania Cassels (née Wetherall), Sandford, Scotland
Jane Chander, Hemel Hempstead
Jean Chapman, Edale
Aimee Code, Edale, Derbyshire
Josephine Code, Edale, Derbyshire
Charles Coghlan
Mrs J.S.E. Coghlan, Upton-upon-Severn, Worcestershire
Lucinda Coghlan
John and Margaret Connors, Glen Tor, Edale
G. Bryan Cooper, Chinley, High Peak
Harold C. Cooper, Great Asby, Cumbria
Norman Cooper, Chapel-en-le-Frith/ formerly Edale
Mr Roger M. Cooper, Edale, Derbyshire
Roy and Gwen Cooper, Highfield Farm, Edale
Ronan Corrigan, Luddenden, West Yorkshire
Richard Crabtree, Baslow, Derbyshire
Andrew and Anita, Callum and Elspeth Critchlow, Edale
Raymond and Belinda (née Heardman) Critchlow, Edale

Margaret Crofts (née Eyre), Codsall, Staffordshire
Jacqueline Crookes (née Cooper), Scotland
Keith E. Dakin, Queensland, Australia
May Davis, formerly of Edale
Anne C. Dobbin, Stockport, Cheshire
Gary J. Dobbin, Hollinwood, Oldham
Kevin J. Douglas, Mill Hill, London
Adrian Earp
Mr Gary James Elliott, Northampton
James Clarke Elliott, Edale, Derbyshire
Mr Jack Elmore, Gleadless, Town End, Sheffield
Fairlie Elrington, Edale House, Edale
Gladys Emery, Bradwell, Derbyshire
Mr and Mrs Eric Emsen, Worcester
Anthony Favell and Susan Favell
Mr and Mrs R.D. France, Woodlands
Cynthia French, Woodthorpe, Nottingham
Mrs Val Gilbert, Nether Booth Farm, Edale
J.B. Glanville, Mill Cottages, Edale
Michael and Karen Green (née Howe), St Albans, Hertfordshire
Nigel Green, Edale, Derbyshire
Harold Gregory, Glossop, Derbyshire
Richard and Kay Gregory, Hartington, Derbyshire
Peter C. Harrison, Castleton, Derbyshire
James Heardman, Edinburgh
Milly Heardman, Edale
Robert and Sarah Helliwell, Edale, Derbyshire
E. Hickinson
John and Sue Hickinson, Glossop, Derbyshire
Ruby and Philip Hicks, Edale, Derbyshire
T.W. Hill, Manor House Farm, Edale
Holly Primary School, Forest Town, Mansfield

SUBSCRIBERS

Edna M. Hopcroft (née Critchlow), Kegworth, Derbyshire
R.H. Horn, New Mills, Derbyshire
Rosamond Hough (née Rowbottom)
Mr Desmond V. Howe, Edale, Derbyshire
Mr and Mrs C.W. Hulse
Leslie and Ella Inskip, Edale, Derbyshire
Caroline and Rob Jackson, Edale
Mr C. Jackson, Edmonton, Alberta, Canada
Morgan Jackson, Edale
Dr and Mrs S.H. Jackson
Simon and Jana Jackson, Edale
Tony Jackson, Chapel-en-le-Frith, Derbyshire
Carol Jamieson and Richard Grimes
James Littlewood Hadfield, born Edale 1844
Mrs Elizabeth Longdon (née Cooper), Chapel-en-le-Frith, High Peak
John A. Longden, Chapel-en-le-Frith, Derbyshire
V. Loomes, Hathersage, Hope Valley
Julian May, Wotton-under-Edge, Gloucestershire
June Mayers (née Eyre), born Hope Road, Edale, 1936
S. and S. McGinity (née Longdon), Pukekohe, New Zealand
H. David Mellor, Little Hayfield, Derbyshire
Robin Metcalfe, Smallclough, Edale, Derbyshire
Norah M. Midgley, Shatton, Hope Valley
Gordon Miller, Edale, Derbyshire
Paddy Mitchell, Derby. Daughter of Madge Cooper
June Morris
Margaret Mountford, Edale
Mr Harry Newton
Mr John and Mrs Glenys Nield, Whitmore Lea Farm, Edale
David N. Noblett, Chinley, High Peak
Mrs Caroline P. Noel, Grindslow House, Edale
A. and E. O'Riley (née Lowe), Chapel-en-le-Frith, High Peak
Amanda Oakes, Rusholme, Manchester
Catherine Parker and Mark Wallington, Edale
Joan M. Pass, Ystumten, Aberystwyth
John Payne, Edale, Derbyshire
Margaret Plant, Spalding
Richard, Annamarie and Joseph Plant, Lichfield
David W. Price, Hope, Derbyshire
Linda Read
Julia Reid, Edale, Derbyshire
E. Robinson, Castleton, Derbyshire
Rosie Rumble, Edale
W. Stephen B. Sampson, Bamford, Derbyshire
Mr Joseph and Miss Patricia Shirt, Hope, Derbyshire
Christopher D. Sims, Wortegem-Petegem, Belgium
Mr and Mrs F. Sims, Kingaroy, Australia
Mr and Mrs R. Sims, Ollerton, Notts.
Jean and Ken Slack, Sheffield
Joyce Sledger (Gibbons), Richmond, North Yorkshire
Smith, Dale Head Farm, and Harris, The Lea
Professor Roderick A. Smith, London
Stella Smith, Chinley, Derbyshire
Staffordshire University, Geography Department
Philip and Vivienne Taylor, Hope, Derbyshire
Julia Thompson, Edale, Derbyshire
Dr Denise Thwaites-Bee, Edale, Derbyshire
Victoria Turner, Castleton, Derbyshire
Mrs Maud Tym, Chapel-en-le-Frith, Derbyshire
Jill M. Walker, Edale, Derbyshire
Elizabeth and Clive Wetherall, Edale
Jessica Wetherall, Ham, Surrey
Sheila White, Swindon
David Widdowson, York
Ian Widdowson, Buxton
John Widdowson
Lyn Widdowson
Mrs Joyce S. Wilde, Hayfield, High Peak
Irene Wilkinson
Ryan John Wilkinson, Edale, Derbyshire
Pamela J. Williams, Hawkwell, Essex
David Wilson, Carlisle
David Wilson, The Orchard, Edale
Susan L. Wood, Stockport, Cheshire
Terry Woodhouse, Chesterfield, Derbyshire
Margaret Wrenn, Hope, Derbyshire
Chris Wright, Edale, Derbyshire
The Yeardley Family, Edale

Community Histories

The Book of Addiscombe • Canning and Clyde Road Residents Association and Friends
The Book of Addiscombe, Vol. II • Canning and Clyde Road Residents Association and Friends
The Book of Axminster with Kilmington • Les Berry and Gerald Gosling
The Book of Bampton • Caroline Seward
The Book of Barnstaple • Avril Stone
The Book of Barnstaple, Vol. II • Avril Stone
The Book of The Bedwyns • Bedwyn History Society
The Book of Bickington • Stuart Hands
Blandford Forum: A Millennium Portrait • Blandford Forum Town Council
The Book of Bramford • Bramford Local History Group
The Book of Breage & Germoe • Stephen Polglase
The Book of Bridestowe • D. Richard Cann
The Book of Bridport • Rodney Legg
The Book of Brixham • Frank Pearce
The Book of Buckfastleigh • Sandra Coleman
The Book of Buckland Monachorum & Yelverton • Pauline Hamilton-Leggett
The Book of Carharrack • Carharrack Old Cornwall Society
The Book of Carshalton • Stella Wilks and Gordon Rookledge
The Parish Book of Cerne Abbas • Vivian and Patricia Vale
The Book of Chagford • Iain Rice
The Book of Chapel-en-le-Frith • Mike Smith
The Book of Chittlehamholt with Warkleigh & Satterleigh • Richard Lethbridge
The Book of Chittlehampton • Various
The Book of Colney Heath • Bryan Lilley
The Book of Constantine • Moore and Trethowan
The Book of Cornwood and Lutton • Compiled by the People of the Parish
The Book of Creech St Michael • June Small
The Book of Cullompton • Compiled by the People of the Parish
The Book of Dawlish • Frank Pearce
The Book of Dulverton, Brushford, Bury & Exebridge • Dulverton and District Civic Society
The Book of Dunster • Hilary Binding
The Book of Edale • Gordon Miller
The Ellacombe Book • Sydney R. Langmead
The Book of Exmouth • W.H. Pascoe
The Book of Grampound with Creed • Bane and Oliver
The Book of Hayling Island & Langstone • Peter Rogers
The Book of Helston • Jenkin with Carter
The Book of Hemyock • Clist and Dracott
The Book of Herne Hill • Patricia Jenkyns
The Book of Hethersett • Hethersett Society Research Group
The Book of High Bickington • Avril Stone
The Book of Ilsington • Dick Wills
The Book of Kingskerswell • Carsewella Local History Group
The Book of Lamerton • Ann Cole and Friends
Lanner, A Cornish Mining Parish • Sharron Schwartz and Roger Parker
The Book of Leigh & Bransford • Malcolm Scott
The Book of Litcham with Lexham & Mileham • Litcham Historical and Amenity Society
The Book of Loddiswell • Loddiswell Parish History Group
The New Book of Lostwithiel • Barbara Fraser
The Book of Lulworth • Rodney Legg
The Book of Lustleigh • Joe Crowdy
The Book of Lyme Regis • Rodney Legg
The Book of Manaton • Compiled by the People of the Parish
The Book of Markyate • Markyate Local History Society
The Book of Mawnan • Mawnan Local History Group
The Book of Meavy • Pauline Hemery
The Book of Minehead with Alcombe • Binding and Stevens
The Book of Morchard Bishop • Jeff Kingaby
The Book of Newdigate • John Callcut
The Book of Nidderdale • Nidderdale Museum Society
The Book of Northlew with Ashbury • Northlew History Group
The Book of North Newton • J.C. and K.C. Robins
The Book of North Tawton • Baker, Hoare and Shields
The Book of Nynehead • Nynehead & District History Society
The Book of Okehampton • Roy and Ursula Radford
The Book of Paignton • Frank Pearce
The Book of Penge, Anerley & Crystal Palace • Peter Abbott
The Book of Peter Tavy with Cudlipptown • Peter Tavy Heritage Group
The Book of Pimperne • Jean Coull
The Book of Plymtree • Tony Eames
The Book of Porlock • Dennis Corner
Postbridge – The Heart of Dartmoor • Reg Bellamy
The Book of Priddy • Albert Thompson
The Book of Princetown • Dr Gardner-Thorpe
The Book of Rattery • By the People of the Parish
The Book of St Day • Joseph Mills and Paul Annear
The Book of Sampford Courtenay with Honeychurch • Stephanie Pouya
The Book of Sculthorpe • Gary Windeler
The Book of Seaton • Ted Gosling
The Book of Sidmouth • Ted Gosling and Sheila Luxton
The Book of Silverton • Silverton Local History Society
The Book of South Molton • Jonathan Edmunds
The Book of South Stoke with Midford • Edited by Robert Parfitt
South Tawton & South Zeal with Sticklepath • Roy and Ursula Radford
The Book of Sparkwell with Hemerdon & Lee Mill • Pam James
The Book of Staverton • Pete Lavis
The Book of Stithians • Stithians Parish History Group
The Book of Stogumber, Monksilver, Nettlecombe & Elworthy • Maurice and Joyce Chidgey
The Book of Studland • Rodney Legg
The Book of Swanage • Rodney Legg
The Book of Tavistock • Gerry Woodcock
The Book of Thorley • Sylvia McDonald and Bill Hardy
The Book of Torbay • Frank Pearce
The Book of Watchet • Compiled by David Banks
The Book of West Huntspill • By the People of the Parish
Widecombe-in-the-Moor • Stephen Woods
Widecombe – Uncle Tom Cobley & All • Stephen Woods
The Book of Williton • Michael Williams
The Book of Witheridge • Peter and Freda Tout and John Usmar
The Book of Withycombe • Chris Boyles
Woodbury: The Twentieth Century Revisited • Roger Stokes
The Book of Woolmer Green • Compiled by the People of the Parish

For details of any of the above titles or if you are interested in writing your own history, please contact: Commissioning Editor, Community Histories, Halsgrove House, Lower Moor Way, Tiverton Business Park, Tiverton, Devon EX16 6SS, England; email: naomic@halsgrove.com